LIFE OF
OLIVER CROMWELL

ROBERT SOUTHEY

Published by Left of Brain Books

Copyright © 2021 Left of Brain Books

ISBN 978-1-396-32158-0

First Edition

All rights reserved. No part of this publication may be reproduced, distributed, or transmitted in any form or by any means, including photocopying, recording, or other electronic or mechanical methods, without the prior written permission of the publisher, except in the case of brief quotations embodied in critical reviews and certain other noncommercial uses permitted by copyright law. Left of Brain Books is a division of Left of Brain Onboarding Pty Ltd.

LIFE OF CROMWELL.[1]

THE pedigree of the Protector's family commences about the middle of the eleventh century with Glothyan lord of Powys, who married Morveth the daughter and heiress of Edwyn ap Tydwell, lord of Cardigan;—a Welsh genealogist no doubt would be able to trace the lords of Cardigan and Powys up to Cadwallader and so on to Brennus and Belinus. William ap Yevan, the representative of the family in the fifteenth century, was in the service first of Jasper duke of Bedford, Henry the seventh's uncle, afterward of that king himself. His son, Morgan Williams, married the sister of that Cromwell whose

---

[1] 1. "Histoire de Cromwell, d'après les Mémoires du Temps et les Recueils Parlementaires." Par M. Villemain. 2 tom. 8vo. Paris, 1819.—2. "Memoirs of the Protector, Oliver Cromwell, and of his Sons Richard and Henry. Illustrated by Original Letters, and other Family Papers." By Oliver Cromwell, Esq., a Descendant of the Family. With Portraits from Original Pictures. London, 1820. 4to.—3. "Oliver Cromwell and his Times." By Thomas Cromwell. London, 1821.—4. "Cromwelliana. A Chronological Detail of Events in which Oliver Cromwell was engaged from the year 1642 to his Death 1658: with a Continuation of other Transactions to the Restoration." Westminster, 1810. Folio.

The first of these works is in all respects a very good book; the second, which contains much less original matter than we had hoped to find there, is the commendable attempt of an old and respectable gentleman to vindicate the character of his great ancestor. Mr. Thomas Cromwell, the author of the third work, appears *not* to be a descendant of the family: his book, though very inferior to M. Villemain's, and composed in too ambitious a style, is on the whole so fairly written and intended, that we advise the author to ask himself whether some of his statements are not more conformable to the prejudices with which he took up the subject, than to the facts with which he became acquainted in pursuing it—to reconsider the grounds and the consistency of some of his opinions—and if a second edition of his book should be called for, to introduce it by a preface somewhat more modest and decorous. The fourth and last article consists of a series of extracts from the Diurnalls, and other publications of those times. With these works before us, and with the aid of such other materials as the rich memoirs of that disastrous age afford, and the industry of later writers has supplied (among whom Mr. Noble deserves especial mention as one of the most laborious and accurate and useful of the pioneer class), we shall endeavor to present a compendious and faithful account of Oliver Cromwell's eventful life.

name is conspicuous in the history of the Reformation, and who, though not irreproachable for his share in the transactions of a portentous reign, is on the whole largely entitled to commiseration and respect. The eldest son of this marriage called himself Richard Cromwell, *alias* Williams, and as the former was the more popular and distinctive name, the *alias*, though long retained by the family in their deeds and wills, was dropped in ordinary use. This Richard was one of the six challengers who held a tournament in 1540 at Westminster against all comers. The justs were proclaimed in France, Flanders, Spain, and Scotland. The challengers entered the field richly accoutred, and their horses trapped in white velvet; the knights and gentlemen who rode before them were apparelled in velvet and white sarsnet, and their servants were all in white doublets, and "hosen out after the Burgonian fashion."[2] Sir Richard was knighted on the second day, and performed his part in the justs so well that the king cried out to him, "formerly thou wast my Dick, but hereafter thou shalt be my diamond;" and then dropping a diamond ring from his finger bade him take it, and ever after bear such a one in the fore gamb of the demy-lion in his crest. As a further proof of the royal favor, he and each of the challengers had a house and a hundred marks annually, to them and their heirs for ever, granted out of the property of the knights of Rhodes, the last prior of that religion dying at this time broken-hearted for the dissolution of his order.

Sir Richard Cromwell was one of those persons who were enriched by the spoils of the church. He was appointed one of the visiters of the religious houses, and received for bis reward so large a portion of the plunder, that the church lands which he had possessed in Huntingdonshire only, were let in Charles the Second's reign for more than £30,000 a year; and besides these he had very great estates in the adjoining counties of Cambridge, Bedford, Rutland, and Northampton. The donors of estates to monasteries and churches usually inserted in their deeds of gift a solemn imprecation against all persons who should usurp the property so bequeathed, or convert it to other purposes than those for which it was consecrated. Though this proved no defence for the estates which had been piously disposed, it was long believed by the people that the property sacrilegiously obtained at the dissolution carried a curse with it; and, in a great majority of instances, the facts were such as to strengthen the

---

[2] Stow, by Howes, ed. 1631, p. 579.

opinion. Without consigning the rapacious courtiers of that age to the bottomless pit, "there to be tormemted for ever with Korah, Dathan, and Abiram, and with Judas Iscariot," it may safely be said that no conscientious man would have taken property clogged with such an entail.

Henry, the eldest son and heir of Sir Richard, was knighted by Queen Elizabeth, who esteemed him highly, and honored him by sleeping at his seat, once the nunnery, at Hinchinbrook, on her return from visiting Cambridge. He was called the golden knight for his wealth and for his liberality, which was of a splendid kind; for, dividing his time between Hinchinbrook and Ramsey, whenever he returned to the latter place he used to throw large sums of money to the poor townsmen. The death of his second wife was one of the alleged crimes for which the witches of Warboys were accused and executed; the property of these poor wretches, amounting to 40*l.*, was forfeited to Sir Henry as lord of the manor, and he gave it to the corporation of Huntingdon on condition that they should procure from Queen's College, Cambridge, every year on lady-day, a doctor or bachelor of divinity to preach in that town against the sin of witchcraft. That condition was regularly fulfilled about fifty years ago: in what manner it is performed at present we know not. Robert, the second son of Sir Henry, was the father of Oliver, so named after his uncle, the head of the family. That uncle, Sir Oliver, was a magnificent personage, for whose expenses even the enormous property which he inherited proved inadequate.

Sir Henry left his younger sons estates of about 300*l.*, a year each: those to which Robert Cromwell succeeded lay in and near the town of Huntingdon, having chiefly or wholly belonged to the Augustinian Monastery of St. Mary. The house in which he resided was either part of the hospital of St. John, or built upon the site and with materials from its ruins. He married Elizabeth, daughter of William Steward, of the city of Ely, a family which, it is not doubted, was allied to the royal house of Scotland. She was the widow of a Mr. Lynne, and is supposed to have brought him little other fortune than her jointure. They had ten children; Oliver was the second, and the only one of the three boys who lived to grow up. Mr. Cromwell was member for his own borough of Huntingdon in the parliament held in the 35th of Elizabeth [1592-3], and he was in the commission of the peace. This satisfied all his ambition: but, to provide for so large a family, he entered into a large brewing business; it was carried on by servants, and Mrs. Cromwell inspected their accounts, which rendered her better able to conduct the business for herself[3] after her husband's death in 1617. Oliver was born April 25, 1599. A nonjuror, who afterward purchased and inhabited the house, used, when he showed the room in which the protector was born, to observe that the devil was behind the door, alluding to a figure of Satan in the hangings. It is said, on the authority of the same person, who was curious in collecting what traditions remained concerning so eminent a man, that Oliver, when an infant, was in as much danger from a great monkey as Gulliver was at Brobdignag. At his grandfather's house one of these mischievous creatures took him out of the cradle, carried him upon the leads of the house, to the dreadful alarm of the family (who made beds and blankets ready, in the forlorn hope of catching him), and at last brought him safely down. He was saved from drowning in his youth by Mr. Johnson, the curate of Cunnington.

Oliver was educated at the free grammar-school of his native town, by Dr. Beard,[4] whose severity toward him is said to have been more than what was usual even in that age of barbarous school-disciple. He was a resolute, active boy, fond of engaging in hazardous exploits, and more capable of hard study

---

[3] Mr. O. Cromwell says, "All this has been said by Cromwell's enemies, for the purpose of degrading him; but no evidence to be relied on is produced in support of these assertions. The truth is, nothing certain is likely to be known of his early life, or the pecuniary circumstances of his parents." "And," he adds, "that, as Cromwell, in a speech to his Parliament, said he was a gentleman, neither living in any considerable height, nor yet in obscurity, such an account of himself is a sufficient confutation of his and his family's narrow circumstances, and their engagements in trade in consequence." This gentlemen very justly observes that the statement, "if true, could not be deemed discreditable to the family, the youngest brothers of the best families in this country engaging in trade and thereby raising themselves to fortune and independency." With this feeling there is an inconsistency in resenting the statement as a wrong. Of such facts no other proof is possible than contemporary assertions, uncontradicted at the time; these are so numerous that it is almost absurd to question them; and what renders the fact highly probable is, that Mrs. Cromwell lived in a very handsome, frugal manner, and gave each of her daughters fortune sufficient to marry them to persons of genteel families;" which she could never have done from her dowry alone, being only 60*l*. a year.

[4] The frontispiece to the Theatre of God's Judgments is said to be a portrait of this severe schoolmaster. It represents him with two scholars standing behind, a rod in his hand, and *As in præsenti* proceeding from his mouth.

than inclined to it. His ambition was of a different kind, and that peculiar kind discovered itself even in his youth. He is said to have displayed a more than common emotion in playing the part of Tactus who finds a royal robe and a crown, in the old comedy of Lingua. The comedy was certainly performed at the free-school of Huntingdon in his time, and if Oliver played the part, the scene in question is one which he must have remembered with singular feeling, whatever he may have felt in enacting it.

> "Was ever man so fortunate as I,
> To break his shins at such a stumbling-block!
> Roses and bays pack hence! this crown and robe
> My brows and body circles and invests.
> How gallantly it fits me. Sure the slave
> Measured my head that wrought this coronet.
> They lie that say complexions can not change;
> My blood's ennobled, and I am transformed
> Unto the sacred temper of a king.
> Methinks I hear my noble parasites
> Styling me Cæsar or great Alexander,
> Licking my feet, and wondering where I got
> This precious ointment. How my pace is mended!
> How princely do I speak, how sharp I threaten!—
> Peasants, I'll curb your headstrong impudence,
> And make you tremble when the lion roars,
> Ye earth-bred worms!—
> Poets will write whole volumes of this change"[5]

He himself is said often, in the height of his fortune, to have mentioned a gigantic figure which, when he was a boy, opened the curtains of his bed, and told him he should be the greatest person in the kingdom. Such a dream he

---

[5] Dodsley's old plays, ed. 1825, vol. v., p. 114. The first edition of "Lingua," a play attributed to Anthony Brewer, is dated 1607. That Cromwell had acted a part in this play, we are told by Simon Miller, a stationer, in a list of publications appended to Heath's New Book of Royal Martyrs. This Heath wrote the earliest printed Life of Oliver Cromwell, entitled "Flagellum, or the Life and Death and Birth and Burial of Oliver Cromwell the late Usurper." (1663). Miller was the publisher of an edition of "Lingua" in 1657, and may have had his information from Heath.

may very probably have had; and nothing can be more likely than that he should seek to persuade himself it was a prophetic vision, when events seemed to place the fulfilment within his reach. But that his Uncle Steward told him it was traitorous to relate it, and that he was flogged for his relation by Dr. Beard, at his father's particular desire, are additions to the story which are disproved by their absurdity; however loyal his parents, and however addicted to the use of the rod his master, they would no more have punished him at that time for such a fancy, than for dreaming that he was to become Grand Turk or Prester John. There is another tale concerning his childhood, which, as well as all these anecdotes, the living historian of the family treats as an absolute falsehood; that being at his uncle's house at Hinchinbrook, when the royal family rested there on their way from Scotland, in 1604, he was brought to play with Prince Charles, then duke of York,[6] quarrelled with him, beat him, and made his noise bleed profusely—which was remembered as a bad omen for the king when Cromwell began to distinguish himself in the civil wars. Mr. Noble relates this only as the tradition of the place, adding that Hinchinbrook was generally one of the resting-places of the royal family on the northern road. Such anecdotes relating to such a man, even though they may be of doubtful authenticity, are not unworthy of preservation. The fabulous history of every country is a part of its history, and ought not to be omitted by later and more enlightened historians; because it has been believed at one time, and while it was believed it influenced the imagination, and thereby, in some degree, the opinions and the character of the people. Biographical fables, on the other hand, are worthy of notice, because they show in what manner the celebrity of the personage, in whose honor or dishonor they have been invented, has acted upon his countrymen. Moreover, there is in the curiosity which we feel concerning the earliest actions of remarkable men, an interest akin to that which is attached to the source of a great river. There are many springs in this country more beautiful in themselves and in their accompaniments than the fountains of the Thames, or the Danube, or the Nile, but how inferior in kind and in degree is the feeling which they excite!

---

[6] Among Prince Henry's expenses is a "payment of xxxiii^{li}. for three Hawkes bought of Sir Oliver Cromwell."

Before Cromwell had quite completed his seventeenth year, he was removed from the school at Huntingdon to Sydney Sussex College, Cambridge.[7] Though his passion for athletic exercises still continued, so much so that he is said to have acquired the name of a royster in the university, it appears certain, that the short time which he passed there was not mispent, but that he made a respectable proficiency in his studies. He had not, however, been there more than a year when his father died, and his mother, to whose care he appears to have been left, removed him from college. It has been affirmed that he was placed at Lincoln's Inn, but that instead of attending to the law he wasted his time "in a dissolute course of life, and good-fellowship and gaming." His descendant denies this, because his name is not to be found in the records of Lincoln's Inn to which sufficient disproof he adds, that "it is not likely a youth of eighteen or nineteen should in those days have been sent to an inn of court." The unlikelihood is not apparent; there is no imaginable reason why he should have been represented as a student of law if he had never been so, and the probability is that he was entered at some other of the inns of court. Returning thence to reside upon his paternal property, he is said to have led a low and boisterous life; and for proof of this, a letter to his cousin, Mrs. St. John, is quoted, in which he says,—"You know what my manner of life hath been. Oh, I lived in and loved darkness, and hated the light; I was a chief, the chief of sinners. This is true; I hated godliness, yet God had mercy on me." The present Mr. Oliver Cromwell argues that no such meaning is to be inferred from the words, but that such "it is conceived would be the language of any person of the present day, who, after professing Christianity in the common loose way in which it is commonly professed, and even preserving themselves free from the commission of all gross sins and immoral acts, should become a convert to the stricter doctrines and precepts of the Scriptures, as held by those who are deemed to be the evangelical or orthodox believers of these times." Mr. Cromwell is right; the letter proves nothing, except that there is a good deal of the same canting now that there was then, cant indeed being a coin which always passes current. The language of an evangelical professor concerning his own sins and the sense of his own wickedness, is no more to be taken literally than that of an amorous sonnetteer who complains of flames and torments.

---

[7] 23d April, 1616. Noble, i. 254, ed. 1787.

The course of Cromwell's conduct, however, at this time was such as to offend his paternal uncle, Sir Oliver, and his maternal one, Sir Thomas Steward. The offence given to the former is said to have been by a beastly frolic, for which the master of Misrule very properly condemned him to the discipline of a horsepond. The story, from its very filthiness, is incredible: Bates, however, would not have related it unless he had believed it, and Oliver's practical jests were sometimes dirty as well as coarse. The means by which he displeased Sir Thomas are less doubtful and of a blacker die:— wishing to get possession of his estate, he represented him as not able to govern it, and petitioned for a commission of lunacy against him, which was refused. Because Sir Thomas was reconciled to him afterward, and ultimately left him the estate, the present Mr. O. Cromwell denies the fact, saying, "This supposed attempt to deprive his uncle of his estate would have been so atrocious and unpardonable, that the reasonable conclusion must be, that this disposition in favor of Cromwell proves the falsehood of the story." A better ground of defence would have been to maintain that the uncle was not in his sound senses, and to allege the bequest, after such provocation, in proof of it. The story is most certainly true; it is established by a speech of Archbishop Williams to the king concerning Cromwell, wherein he says, "Your majesty did him but justice in refusing his petition against Sir Thomas Steward of the isle of Ely; but he takes them all for his enemies that would not let him undo his best friend." Mr. O. Cromwell has overlooked this evidence. But he is not the only modern biographer who has thought proper to contradict the facts which are recorded of an ancestor, because it is not agreeable to believe them. The probability is, that Cromwell, who was not naturally a wicked man, thought his petition well grounded.

Whatever may have been the follies and vices of his youth, it is certain that he had strength and resolution enough to shake them off. As soon as he came of age he married[8] Elizabeth, daughter of Sir James Bourchier, of Felsted, in Essex, a woman whose irreproachable life might have protected her from obloquy and insult, if in the heat of party-spirit anything were held sacred. She brought him some fortune, and, in the year 1625, he was returned to King Charles's first parliament for the borough of Huntingdon. There was no

---

[8] 20th August, 1620. In the church of St. Giles, Cripplegate, the church in which Milton is buried. Noble, i. 123.

disaffection in his family either to the church or state; they had indeed enjoyed in a peculiar manner, the bounty as well as the favor of the crown. But Cromwell was not likely to behold the measures of the government with indifference or complacency; a man so capable of governing well perceived the errors which were committed; and the displeasure thus reasonably excited, was heightened by accidental and personal circumstances till it became a rooted disaffection. To this some of his family connexions must have contributed in no slight degree. Hampden was his first cousin; and St John, who was connected with the Cromwells by his first marriage, married for his second wife one who stood in the same degree of near relationship to him. They were unquestionably two of the ablest men in that distinguished age; and Hampden, who had sagacity enough to perceive the talents of his kinsman when they were not suspected by others, possessed a great influence over his mind; Cromwell "followed his advice while living, and revered his memory when dead." These eminent men were both deadly enemies at heart to the established church, and the puritanical bias which their conversation was likely to impart was increased by his own disposition, for in the early part of his life it is certain that he was of a fanatical constitution. He often supposed himself to be dying, and called up his physician at unseasonable hours in causeless alarm; and that physician's account of him is, that "he was quite a splenetic, and had fancies about the Cross in the town."[9]

Cromwell sat for the same borough in the parliament of 1628, and spoke severely and justly against the promotion of Dr. Manwaring; but by complaining at the same time of persons who "preached flat popery," which was a flat falsehood, he lessened the effect of his opinion upon unprejudiced and judicious minds. Three years afterward he sold some of his estates for 1800*l.*; stocked a grazing farm at St. Ives, and removed thither from Huntingdon. The barn which he built here was still standing, and bore his name, when Mr. Noble published his Memoirs of the Protectoral House;[10] and the farmer who then rented the estate marked his sheep with the identical marking irons which Oliver used, and which had O. C. upon them.[11] While he resided here he returned some money which he had formerly won by

---

[9] Sir Philip Warwick's Memoirs, ed. 1702, p. 249.
[10] The first edition of Noble's memoirs was published in 1784.
[11] Noble, i. 262.

gaming, and which he considered it sinful to keep. The sums were not inconsiderable for that time and for his means, one of them being 30*l.* and another 120*l.* The death of Sir Thomas Steward placed him in affluence, and, in 1635, he removed to the Glebe House in the city of Ely. He had now a large family, and took his full share in local business as an active country gentleman, not always as a useful one, for the scheme of draining the fens of Lincolnshire and the isle of Ely, which his father and many others of his relations had promoted, was defeated chiefly by his opposition. There was a popular cry against the measure, because the inhabitants enjoyed a customary right of commoning and fishing there; Cromwell therefore became so great a favorite with them for espousing their immediate interest, that he was called the Lord of the Fens. It is more likely that he was actuated by a desire of ingratiating himself with the people of the country on this occasion, than that so far-sighted and able a man should not have perceived the great and obvious utility of the measure which he resisted. Afterward, when the act passed under the commonwealth, he was appointed one of the commissioners; and the work proceeded with his favor when he was Protector.

The state of England, though the country was rapidly improving, and prosperous beyond all former example, was such as might well trouble every upright and thoughtful observer. The wisest man could not possibly foresee in what the conflict of opinions, which had begun, was likely to terminate: this only was certain, that there must inevitably be great evil in the process, and that whatever extreme prevailed, the end must needs be one which no good man, or true friend of his country, could contemplate without sorrow. In any other age, Charles I. would have been the best and the most popular of kings. His unambitious and conscientious spirit would have preserved the kingdom in peace; his private life would have set an example of dignified virtue, such as had rarely been seen in courts; and his love of arts and letters would have conferred permanent splendor upon his age, and secured for himself the grateful applause of after generations. But he succeeded to a crown whose prerogatives had been largely asserted and never defined; to a scanty revenue, and to a popular but expensive war, no wise honorable to the nation either in its cause or conduct. The history of his reign thus far had been a series of errors and faults on all sides, so that an impartial observer would have found it difficult to satisfy himself whether the king and his ministers or the parliaments were the most reprehensible; or which party had given the greatest provocation, and thereby afforded most excuse for the conduct of the other. Unable to govern with a parliament, and impatient of being governed by one, Charles had tried the perilous experiment of governing without one. There can be no doubt that the liberties of Great Britain must have been destroyed if that experiment had been successful; and successful in all human probability it would have been, if a spirit of religious discord had not possessed the nation. For though the system of Charles's administration was arbitrary, and therefore tyrannical, the revenue which he raised by extraordinary means was not greater than what would cheerfully have been granted him in the ordinary and just course of government; it was frugally administered, and applied in a manner suitable to the interest and honor of the kingdom, which, for twelve years, in the words of Lord Clarendon, "enjoyed the greatest calm and the fullest measure of felicity that any people in any age, for so long time together, have been blessed with, to the wonder and envy of all the other parts of Christendom." Foreign and domestic trade flourished and increased; towns grew, not with a forced and unhealthy growth, occasioned by the unnatural activity of a manufacturing system, but in just proportion to the growing industry and wealth of the country. England was respected abroad and prosperous at home; it even seemed as if the physical condition of the island had undergone a beneficial change, for the visitations of pestilence were abating, which had been so frequent in the preceding reign. But a severer judgment was impending over a headstrong generation, insensible of the blessings with which they were favored, and ungrateful for them.

While this long calm endured, the most sagacious politicians were so far from perceiving any indications of the storm which they were to direct, that, believing the country was doomed and resigned to the loss of its liberties, they resolved upon leaving it, and transporting themselves, in voluntary exile, to a land of freedom. Lord Brooke, Lord Say and Sele and his sons, Pym, and other distinguished men of the same sentiments, were about to remove to a settlement in New England, where the name of Saybrooke, in honor of the two noble leaders, had already been given to a township in which they were expected. Eight vessels, with emigrants on board were ready to sail from the Thames, when the king by an order of council forbade their departure, and compelled the intended passengers to come on shore, fatally for himself; for among those passengers Haslerigge and Hampden, and Cromwell, with all his family, had actually embarked. There are few facts in history which have so much the appearance of fatality as this.

Charles and his ministers feared that so many discontented and stirring spirits would be perilous in a colony which, being decidedly hostile to the church of England, might easily be alienated from the state. They saw clearly the remote danger, but they were blind to the nearer and greater evil; and in that error they stopped the issue which the peccant humors had opened for themselves. Cromwell returned to Ely, and there continued to lead a respectable and pious life. A letter which he wrote at this time to Mrs. St. John (already mentioned) has been preserved; it is better expressed than most of his compositions, and is remarkable, not merely for its characteristic language, but for a passage which may perhaps be thought to imply the hope, if not the expectation, of making himself conspicuous in defence of his religious sentiments. "Dear Cousin," he says, "I thankfully acknowledge your love in your kind remembrance of me upon this opportunity. Alas, you do too highly prize my lines, and my company; I may be ashamed to own your expressions, considering how unprofitable I am and the mean improvement of my talent. Yet to honor my God by declaring what he hath done for my soul, in this I am confident, and I will be so. Truly then this I find, that he giveth springs in a dry and barren wilderness, where no water is. I live (you know where) in Mesheck, which they say signifies prolonging; in Kedar, which signifieth blackness: yet the Lord forsaketh me not. Though he do prolong, yet he will, I trust, bring me to his tabernacle, to his resting-place. My soul is with the congregation of the first born: my body rests in hope; *and if here I may honor my God, either by doing or suffering, I shall be more glad. Truly no poor creature hath more cause to put forth himself in the cause of his God than I.* I have had plentiful wages before hand, and I am sure I shall never earn the least mite. The Lord accept me in his Son, and give me to walk in the light, and give us to walk in the light, as he is in the light: He it is that enlighteneth our blackness, our darkness. I dare not say he hideth his face from me; he giveth me to see light in his light. One beam in a dark place hath exceeding much refreshment in it; blessed be his name for shining upon so dark a heart as mine!"

This readiness *to do* and *to suffer* in a righteous cause might have been confined to the ignoble theatre of a bishop's court, if a wider field had not soon been opened for puritanical ambition. Cromwell had usually attended the church-service, joining probably, like Baxter, "in the common prayer, with as hearty fervency, as afterward he did with other prayers:"—"As long as I had no prejudice against it," says that good man, "I had no stop in my devotions from any of its imperfections." But even before he left Huntingdon his house had been a retreat for those non-conforming preachers who had provoked the law; and a building behind it is shown, which he is said to have erected for their use, and in which, according to the same tradition, he sometimes edified them by a discourse himself. It is certain that he put himself forward in their cause so as to be looked upon as the head of their party in that country; and Williams, who was then bishop of Lincoln, and whom he often troubled on such occasions, says that he was a common spokesman for sectaries, and maintained their part with stubbornness. Whatever part indeed Cromwell took up would be well maintained, and the time was now approaching when he was to take a conspicuous one.

A rebellion broke out in Scotland, where no disaffection had been suspected. By prudent measures it might easily have been averted, by vigorous ones it might easily have been crushed; and both were wanting. The king raised an army which, by the management of designing persons, and the mismanagement of others, was rendered useless. A treaty was made by which nothing was concluded; all the savings of the preceding years were wasted in this disgraceful expedition; and Charles, who had so long governed without a parliament, was now compelled to call one, for the purpose of obtaining supplies. The majority of that parliament consisted of men who knew their duty to their king and country, and, in asserting the constitutional liberties of the people, would have sacredly preserved the rights of the crown; wherein those liberties have their surest safeguard. There were however some persons, of great ability, who were determined upon effecting some change both in the ecclesiastic and civil institutions of the land, not having acknowledged to others, nor perhaps to themselves, how far they were willing that that change should extend. The state of their mind was well expressed by Cromwell, who, when Sir Thomas Chichley and Sir Philip Warwick asked him with what concessions he would be satisfied, honestly replied, "I can tell you, sirs, what I would not have, though I can not tell what I would." This parliament was hastily dissolved by the counsel of Sir Henry Vane the elder, and Herbert the solicitor-general: the latter acted with no worse motives than peevishness and mortified pride; the former appears to have intended the mischief which ensued. The discontented party did not conceal their joy at an event which made all good men mournful. Cromwell's cousin St. John, whose dark and treacherous spirit at all other times clouded his countenance, met Mr. Hyde with a smiling and cheerful aspect, and seeing him melancholy, "as in truth be was from his heart," asked what troubled him. The same, he replied, which troubled most good men, that in such a time of confusion, so wise a parliament, which alone could have found remedy for it, was so unseasonably dismissed. But St. John warmly made answer, that all was well: and that it must be worse before it was better: and that this parliament could never have done what was necessary to be done—"as indeed," says Hyde, "it would not what he and his friends thought necessary." Cromwell was one of those friends; he had been returned to this parliament for the town of Cambridge, and was returned for the same seat to the next—the famous and infamous Long Parliament, which Charles found it necessary to call in six months after the dissolution.

Cromwell's appearance in this assembly is happily described by Sir Philip Warwick. "The first time," he says, "that ever I took notice of him, was in the very beginning of the parliament held in November, 1640,[12] when I vainly thought myself a courtly young gentleman, for we courtiers valued ourselves much upon our good clothes. I came one morning into the house well clad, and perceived a gentleman speaking, whom I knew not, very ordinarily apparelled, for it was a plain cloth suit, which seemed to have been made by an ill country tailor. His linen was plain, and not very clean; and I remember a speck or two of blood upon his little band, which was not much larger than his collar: his hat was without a hat-band; his stature was of a good size; his sword stuck close to his side, his countenance swollen and reddish, his voice sharp and untunable, and his eloquence full of fervor."[13] But it was more by heat and earnestness than by eloquence that Cromwell made himself noticed at this time. One of the first occasions upon which he spoke in this parliament was in a, committee, in opposition to Lord Kimbolton, upon the earl of Manchester's enclosure

---

[12] He sat in this parliament—commonly known as the Long Parliament—for the town of Cambridge. His fellow-member was John Lawry, Esq.

[13] Sir Philip Warwick's Memoirs, ed. 1702, p. 247.

business. He behaved intemperately, "ordering the witnesses and petitioners in the method of proceeding, and seconding, and enlarging upon what they said with great passion."[14] When the chairman endeavored to preserve order, by speaking with authority, Cromwell accused him of being partial and discountenancing the witnesses; and when, says Lord Clarendon, who was himself the chairman, Lord Kimbolton, "upon any mention of matter of fact, or the proceeding before and at the enclosure, desired to be heard, and with great modesty related what had been done, or explained what had been said, Mr. Cromwell did answer and reply upon him with so much indecency and rudeness, and in language so contrary and offensive, that every man would have thought, that as their natures and their manners were as opposite as it is possible, so their interest could never have been the same. In the end his whole carriage was so tempestuous, and his behavior so insolent, that the chairman found himself obliged to reprehend him, and to tell him if he proceeded in the same manner, he would presently adjourn the committee, and the next morning complain to the house of him."[15]

Cromwell's name does not appear in the proceedings against Lord Strafford. That he bore his part, however, may be presumed not only from the whole tenor of his after-conduct, but because his cousin St. John was one of the foremost agents in that most iniquitous transaction, one of the deadly sins of the Long Parliament. When the question of the Remonstrance, much against the will of the violent party, was deferred till the morrow, that there might be time for debating it, Cromwell asked Lord Falkland why he would have it put off, for that day would quickly have determined it. Lord Falkland answered there would not have been time enough, for sure it would take some debate; and Cromwell replied, a very sorry one for he, and those with whom he acted, supposed there would be little opposition. It was so well opposed that the debate continued from nine in the morning till midnight; a thing at that time wholly unprecedented. As they went out of the house, Lord Falkland asked him, whether there had been a debate. To which Cromwell replied, he would take his word another time, and whispered him in the ear,

---

[14] Lord Clarendon's Life of himself, ed. 1827, vol., i. p. 89.

[15] Which he never forgave; and took all occasions afterward to pursue him with the utmost malice and revenge to his death.—Clar. Life, ed. 1827, vol. i., p. 90.

that if the Remonstrance had been rejected, he would have sold all he had the next morning, and never have seen England more; and he knew there were many other honest men of the same resolution. So near, says Clarendon, was the poor kingdom at that time to its deliverance.[16]

That memorable Remonstrance, which must have been intended by those who framed it to prepare the way for the evils which ensued, was carried (14th Nov., 1641) by a majority of nine, when not half the members of the house were present: the promoters of the measures were so active, that not a man of their party was wanting, and at the last they carried it by the hour of the night, which drove away more old and infirm opposers than would have sufficed to turn the scale. Whitelock says, "the sitting up all night caused many through weakness or weariness to leave the house, and Sir B. R. (Sir Benjamin Rudyard) to compare it to the verdict of a starved jury."[17] What Clarendon observes upon this occasion is worthy of especial notice "I know not how those men have already answered it to their own consciences; or how they will answer it to Him who can discern their consciences; who having assumed their country's trust, and, it may be, with great earnestness labored to procure that trust, by their supine laziness, negligence, and absence, were the first inlets to those inundations; and so contributed to those licenses which have overwhelmed us. For by this means a handful of men, much inferior in the beginning, in number and interest, came to give laws to the major part: and, to show that three diligent persons are really a greater and more significant number than ten unconcerned, they, by plurality of voices in the end, converted or reduced the whole body to their opinions. It is true, men of activity and faction, in any design, have many advantages, that a composed and settled council, though industrious enough, usually have not; and some that gallant men can not give themselves leave to entertain: for besides their thorough considering and forming their counsels before they execute them,

---

[16] Clar. Hist., ed. 1826, vol. ii., p. 44. Lord Say and Lord Brooke were the promoters of this intended emigration, and, as is well known, Hampden and his cousin Cromwell, and Haselrigge, had actually embarked for the new colony of Saybrooke, when an order of council, restraining all masters and owners of ships from setting forth any vessel without special license was enforced against them. *Nescia mens hominum fati sortisque faturæ.*— SOUTHEY, *Quar. Rev.*, No. xciv., p. 478.

[17] Whitelock, p. 51, ed. 1732.

they contract a habit of ill-nature and disingenuity necessary to their affairs, and the temper of those upon whom they are to work, that liberal-minded men would not persuade themselves to entertain, even for the prevention of all the mischief the others intend. And whosoever observes the ill arts by which these men use to prevail upon the people in general; their absurd, ridiculous lying, to win the affections, and corrupt the understandings of the weak; and the bold scandals to confirm the wilful; the boundless promises they presented to the ambitious; and their gross, abject flatteries and applications to the vulgar-spirited, would hardly give himself leave to use those weapons for the preservation of the three kingdoms."[18]

By such means a civil war was brought on; by such weapons the civil and religious establishments of the kingdom were for a season overthrown. The wisest of men has said, "the thing which hath been, it is that which shall be:" and the same means will produce a recurrence of the same evils unless right-minded men learn wisdom from the past. There is no historian, ancient or modern, with whose writings it so much behooves an Englishman to be thoroughly conversant, as Lord Clarendon.

One day when Cromwell had spoken warmly in the house, Lord Digby asked Hampden who he was; and Hampden is said to have replied, "That sloven whom you see before you, hath no ornament in his speech; that sloven, I say, if we should ever come to a breach with the king (which God forbid!) in such a case, I say, that sloven will be the greatest man in England." Baxter has said of Hampden, that he was a man whom "friends and enemies acknowledged to be the most eminent for prudence, piety, and peaceable councils." That he was a man of consummate abilities is certain; that he was eminently pious may be believed, the darkest political intrigues being perfectly compatible with the eminent piety of that age; but no man even in that age had less pretension to be praised for his peaceable councils. Had Hampden died soon after the meeting of the Long Parliament, when he possessed more power to do good or hurt than any person of his rank had ever possessed before him, he would have left a character unimpeached and unimpeachable, and have deservedly held in the hearts of all good and wise men that place which he holds now with those only who know him by name alone, or who

---

[18] Clar. Hist.; vol. ii., p. 57, ed. 1826.

avow their attachment to the cause for which he bled in the field, without being more explicit than is convenient concerning the nature of that cause. His noble stand against an illegal exertion of the prerogative would have entitled him to the everlasting gratitude of his country; and if he could have been contented with defining that prerogative, limiting it within just bounds, redressing the existing grievances, and giving the constitution that character which it obtained after the Revolution, he would have left a memorable name. And this was in his power.

What his views were can only be inferred from the course of his conduct; for he was cut off[19] before the time arrived for openly declaring them. The probable inference is, that like Ireton, Algernon Sidney, and Ludlow, he was a stern republican. Having read of no constitution so happily balanced as that which this country has enjoyed since the Revolution, and seeing nothing like it in our previous history, he may have believed such a balance of power to be unattainable, and therefore have resolved upon endeavoring to introduce a simpler and severer form. On the supposition that the alternative was an absolute monarchy (such as, till his time, the sovereign of this kingdom had claimed, and the parliaments had acknowledged) or a commonwealth, he may have properly and uprightly preferred that polity under which the most security had been enjoyed, the greatest talents had been called forth, and the most splendid exploits had been achieved. But if, upon this fair ground, they who reasoned thus may be justified in wishing for the end at which they aimed, nothing can justify the means by which it was pursued; and in those means no man was more deeply implicated than Hampden. The catholics never more boldly avowed the principle, that any means are lawful for compassing a necessary end, than the puritans acted upon it: even good men of feeble understandings or weak characters, were too easily inveigled into that conclusion; whereas, as their great contemporary historian has justly observed, "the true logic is, that the thing desired is not necessary, if the ways are unlawful which are proposed to bring it to pass."

One set of men were bent upon pulling down episcopacy, though it should occasion as bloody a war as any with which England had ever been afflicted. There were others who knew these men to be knaves, but were willing to act

---

[19] He was mortally wounded in a skirmish on Chalgrove Field, 18th June, 1643.

in concert with them, for the purpose of destroying the monarchy, meaning, when that object should have been effected, to deal with them as they had dealt with others. From the hour of Strafford's arrest they felt their strength, and saw that, by the means which they were prepared to use, success was certain. His arrest had been carried with an overwhelming power, because the great majority of members dreaded the influence of a minister so resolute, so able, and so arbitrary; and therefore with the best intentions voted for it by acclamation. But when that illustrious victim was to be destroyed by measures more flagrantly illegal, and more tyrannical, than the worst actions of which he stood accused, they who had taken upon themselves to raise and to direct the storm well knew that the co-operation of no upright man could be expected. But they knew also where to look for other allies, and how to force most even of those who abhorred their purpose, to act in subservience to it.

> "Craft, go thou forth!
> Fear, make it safe for no man to be just!
> Wrong, be thou clothed in power's comeliness!
> Keep down the best, and let the worst have power!"

They proceeded upon a deliberate system of deceit and intimidation. Free license was given to a libellous press; the pulpits were manned with seditious preachers: they got the management of the city into their hands, by ousting from the common council the grave and substantial citizens, of whom till then it had been composed, and filling their places with men for whom factious activity was deemed sufficient qualification; and by choosing a demagogue lord-mayor, who was ready for any act of rebellion and treason. How easily the populace were to be duped they well understood, and how justly characterized by a dramatist of their own age,—

> "Good silly people; souls that will
> Be cheated without trouble. One eye is
> Put out with zeal, the other with ignorance;
> And yet they think they're eagles!"

They understood also how to act upon the moral weakness of those who were not likely to be deceived. They called the physical force of the city to their aid; and under fear of the mob, senators shrunk from their duty, when they ought rather to have laid down their lives in discharging it. The bishops were wanting to themselves and their order and their king, when, under the influence of fear, they abandoned their right of voting upon the attainder of Strafford: and the lords, when a mob was at the door, and Mr. Hollis (who afterward sat in judgment upon some of his colleagues) desired, in compliance with the demand of that mob, to know the names of those who were opposed to the wishes of the commons, passed, under that intimidation, a bill which they had twice before rejected. The moderate part of the members in that assembly might have outvoted the promoters of rebellion, four to one; but, in fear of their lives, they either left the house or acquiesced in motions which they abhorred. The condition of the house of commons was worse; because there the men of worst intentions, were also the men of greatest ability, "and the number of the weak and wilful," says Clarendon, "who naturally were to be guided by them, always made up a major part: so that from the beginning they were always able to carry whatsoever they set their hearts visibly upon; at least to discredit or disgrace any particular man, against whom they thought necessary to proceed, albeit of the most unblemished reputation, and upon the most frivolous suggestions." They waged war in parliament, as Cromwell did afterward in Ireland, upon the principle of destroying all who opposed them, and the success was the same. At the most important debates there was seldom a fifth part of the members present, and often more than twelve or thirteen in the house lords.

It is especially worthy of notice that the faults for which the king's government was most severely reproached, were committed by the parliament in a far greater degree, and with every possible aggravation. One of the accusations against Charles was that he suffered himself to guided by clerical counsellors; and the argument upon which they chiefly insisted in support of the bill for taking away the bishops' votes in parliament was that "their intermeddling with temporal affairs was inconsistent with, and destructive to, the exercise of their spiritual function;" "while their reformation," it has been truly observed, "both in Scotland and this kingdom, was driven on by no men so much as those of their clergy, who were their instruments; as without doubt the archbishop of Canterbury had never so great an influence upon the councils at court as Dr. Burgess and Mr. Marshal had upon the houses: neither did all the bishops of Scotland together meddle so much in temporal affairs as

Mr. Henderson had done." The breaches of privilege which Charles had committed were represented by them as destructive to the freedom of parliament; and yet their conduct, both to the king and to the house of peers, was an absolute rooting up of all privileges. One of the most unpopular acts of the king had been the levying of ship-money without the consent of the parliament; an impost then only of doubtful legality, yet equally levied, excellently applied, and so light in itself that the payment which Hampden honorably disputed was only twenty shillings upon an estate of 500*l.* a year. The parliament did not scruple, without consent of the king, to demand the twentieth part of every man's property in London, or so much as their seditious mayor and three other persons as seditious as himself might please to call a twentieth, to be levied by distress if the parties refused payment; and if the distress did not cover the assessment, then the defaulter was to be imprisoned where and as long as a committee of the house of commons should think proper, and his family was no longer to remain in London, or the suburbs, or the abjoining counties. With an impudence of slander which would be incredible, if anything were too bad to be believed of thoroughly factious men which will serve their purposes, they accused the king of exciting the massacre in Ireland, and fomenting the rebellion there; and they themselves employed the money and the means which were prepared for quelling that rebellion, in carrying on a war against the king at home.

The king more than once in his declaration reminded them of a speech of Pym's, which they had heard deservedly applauded when it was directed against his measures; but which now bore against their own with greater force. "The law," said that powerful speaker, "is that which puts a difference between good and evil, just and unjust; if you take away the law, all things will be in a confusion; every man will become a law unto himself, which, in the depraved condition of human nature, must needs produce many great enormities. Lust will become a law, and envy will become a law, covetousness and ambition will become laws, and what dictates, what decisions such laws will produce, may easily be discerned:—it may indeed by sad instances over the whole kingdom." And then the king set before them a picture of their own conduct, so ably and so truly drawn, that, if men were governed by their reason and not by their passions, that excellent paper alone would have given the victory over all his enemies. In another declaration the king said "whosoever harbored the least thought in his breast of ruining or violating the public liberty, or religion of the kingdom, let him be accursed; and he should be no counsellor of his that would not say Amen." That which he charged the leaders of parliament with, "was invading the public liberty; and his presumption might be very strong and vehement, that though they had no mind to be slaves, they were not unwilling to be tyrants. What is tyranny," said he, "but to admit no rules to govern by, but their own wills? And they knew the misery of Athens was at the highest, when it suffered under the thirty tyrants." Hobbes, whose resolute way of thinking was more in accord with the temper of Cromwell's government than of the king's, speaks with contempt of these declarations; but if Charles had been served, or known how to serve himself, as ably with the sword as with the pen, the struggle would soon have been decided in his favor. What has been said of the son,[20] that he never said a foolish thing and never did a wise one, might more truly be said of the father: in him, however, it proceeded from what, in other times and other circumstances, would have been a virtue. In speaking, he expressed his own judgment; in acting, he yielded to that of others, and was ruined by want of confidence in himself, and by the fear of doing wrong.

Clarendon, who writes always with the feelings of a Christian, as well as the wisdom of a statesman, has some remarks upon the conduct of the parliament, drawn up with his characteristic candor. "A man shall not unprofitably spend his contemplation, that, upon this occasion, considers the method of God's justice (a method terribly remarkable in many passages, and upon many persons, which we shall be compelled to remember in this discourse), that the same principles, and the same application of those principles, should be used to the wresting all sovereign power from the crown, which the crown had a little before made use of for the extending its authority and power beyond its bounds, to the prejudice of the just rights of the subject. A supposed necessity was then thought ground enough to create a power, and a bare averment of that necessity, to beget a practice to impose what tax they thought convenient upon the subject, by writs of ship-money never before known; and a supposed necessity now, and a bare averment of that necessity, is as confidently, and more fatally, concluded a good ground, to exclude the crown from the use of any

---

[20] By Wilmot Lord Rochester.

power, by an ordinance never before heard of; and the same maxim of *salus populi suprema lex*, which had been used to the infringing the liberty of the one, made use of for the destroying the rights of the other." Reflections of this kind must often have arisen in the mind of Charles himself. When, in his father's lifetime, taking part in Buckingham's animosities, he promoted the impeachment of the earls of Bristol and Middlesex, James said to him, with a foresight which has almost a prophetic character, that he would live to have his belly full of parliamentary impreachments.[21] But he was always more sinned against than sinning: the most unjustifiable of his measures proceeded from a mistaken judgment, not an evil intention; the most unpopular of them, and that which gave the greatest advantage to his enemies (the accusation of the six members), plainly arose from a perfect confidence in his own rectitude, and the goodness of his cause.

The melancholy warning which James gave his son proved the sagacity of that king, whose talents it has been too much the custom to decry. There is an expression of Laud's which bears with it even more of a prophetic appearance, from the accidental turn of the sentence. "At this time, the parliament tendered two, and but two bills to the king to sign: this to cut off Strafford's head was one; and the other was that this parliament should neither be dissolved nor adjourned, but by the consent of both houses: *in which, what he cut off from himself, time will better show than I can.* God bless the king and his royal issue!" Charles's feelings upon that fatal bill which perpetuated the parliament, and thereby in fact transferred the sovereignty to it, are well stated in the Εικων Βασιλικη.[22] "By this act of the highest confidence, I hoped for ever to shut out

---

[21] Clar. Hist., ed. 1826, vol. i., p. 41.

[22] The authenticity of this Book has been attacked and defended with such cogent arguments and strong assertions, that as far as relates to external proofs, perhaps there is scarcely any other question in bibliography so doubtful. The internal evidence is wholly in its favor. Had it been the work of Gauden, or of any person writing to support the royal cause, a higher tone concerning episcopacy and prerogative would have been taken; there would have been more effort at justification; and there would not have been that inefficient but conscientious defence of fatal concessions; that penitent confession of sin where weakness had been sinful; that piety without alloy; that character of mild and even magnanimity; and that heavenly-mindedness, which render the Εικων Βασιλικη one of the most interesting books in our language.

and lock the door upon all present jealousies and future mistakes: I confess I did not thereby intend to shut myself out of doors, as some men have now requited me. A continual parliament, I thought, would but keep the commonweal in tune, by preserving laws in their due execution and vigor, within my interest lies more than any man's, since by those laws my rights as a king would be preserved, no less than my subjects; which is all I desired. More than the law gives me I would not have, and less the meanest subject should not. I can not say properly that I repent of that act, since I have no reflections upon it as a sin of my will, though an error of too charitable a judgment."

Charles appealed to that act with great force as a proof that he had no intention of recurring to arms. "Sure," he says, "it had argued a very short sight of things, and extreme fatuity of mind in me, so far to bind my own hands at their request, if I had shortly meant to use a sword against them." When Hampden spoke of the part which Cromwell might be expected to bear, in case they should come to a breach with the king, he deprecated such an event. But Hampden's studies were rather how to direct a civil war, than to one. Davila's history was so often in his hands, that it was called Colonel Hampden's prayer-book. The truth is, that a few men of daring spirit, great ability, and great popularity, some calling themselves saints because they were schismatics, others styling themselves philosophers because they were unbelievers, had determined to overthrow the existing government in church and state; which they knew to be feasible, because circumstances favored them, and they scrupled at nothing to bring about their end. Their plan was to force from the king all they could, and when they should have disarmed him of all power and means for the struggle, then to provoke him by insults and unreasonable demands, till he should appeal to the sword. This Charles himself saw. "A grand maxim with them was," he says, "always to ask something which in reason and honor must be denied, that they might have some color to refuse all that was in other things granted; setting peace at as high a rate as the worst effects of war; endeavoring first to make me destroy myself by dishonorable concessions, that so they might have the less to do." "The English," says, Hobbes, "would never have taken well

---

[There is a very little testimony on Gauden's side (strictly speaking, perhaps, none at all), except his own . . . . There is a mass of testimony which shows that the king had the book continually in his hand, revised it much, and had many transcripts of it.—SOUTHEY, *Quar. Rev.*, No. lxxiii., p. 249.]

that the parliament should make war upon the king upon any provocation, unless it were in their own defence, in case the king should first make war upon them; and therefore it behooved them to provoke the king, that he might do something that might look like hostility."—"Therefore," he elsewhere adds, "they resolved to proceed with him like skilful hunters, first to single him out by men disposed in all parts, to drive him into the open field, and then in case he should but seem to turn head, to call that a making of war against the parliament."

Never was poor prince more miserably unprepared for such a contest than Charles, when he had no other alternative than to descend into the pit which his enemies had dug for him, or to raise his standard. When that determination was taken he had not "one barrel of gunpowder, nor one musket, nor any other provision necessary for an army; and, which was worse, was not sure of any port, to which they might be securely assigned; nor had he money for the support of his own table for the term of one month." The single ship which reached him with supplies by running ashore, brought about 200 barrels of powder, 2,000 or 3,000 arms, and seven or eight field-pieces; and with this he took the field, but in so helpless and apparently hopeless a condition, that even after he had set up that standard, which was so ominously blown down by a tempest, Clarendon says, it must solely be imputed to his own resolution, that he did not even then go to London and throw himself on the mercy of the parliament, which would have been surrendering at discretion to an enemy that gave no quarter. But he relied upon the goodness of his cause, and upon the loyalty and love of his subjects. That reliance did not deceive him: the gentleman of England came forward with a spirit which enabled him to maintain the contest no inconsiderable time upon equal terms, and which, under the direction of more vigorous counsels, might many times have given him complete success. But it was otherwise appointed. Whoever has attentively perused the history of those unhappy years must have perceived that this war, more perhaps than any other of which the events have been recorded, was determined rather by accidents and blunders, than by foreseen and prepared combinations. The man who most contributed to the king's utter overthrow by his actions, and the only man who from the beginning perceived wherein the strength of the king lay, and by what principle it might be opposed with the surest prospect of success, was Cromwell.

During the proceedings which provoked the war, Cromwell took no conspicuous part, but he was one of that number upon whose votes the leaders of the disaffected party could always rely. He was sincerely a puritan in his religious notions, in that respect more sincere than many of those with whom he then acted: for political speculations he probably cared less; but being a resolute man, and one whose purposes were straight forward, though he frequently proceeded by crooked ways, he, like his cousin Hampden, when he drew the sword, threw away the scabbard. When the war began, he received a captain's commission, and raised a troop of horse in his own country. Then it was that he gave the first proof of that sagacity which made him afterward the absolute master of three kingdoms: in what manner it was now exercised may best be told in his own curious words. "I was a person," said he, "that from my first employment was suddenly preferred and lifted up from lesser trusts to greater, from my first being a captain of a troop of horse; and I did labor as well as I could, to discharge my trust: and God blessed me as it pleased him; and I did truly and plainly; and then in a way of foolish simplicity (as it was judged by very great and wise men, and good men too) desired to make my instruments to help me in this work; and I will deal plainly with you; I had a very worthy friend then, and he was a very noble person, and I know his memory is very grateful to all, Mr. John Hampden. At my first going out into this engagement, I saw their men were beaten at every hand; I did indeed, desired him that he would make some additions to my Lord Essex's army of some new regiments; and I told him I would be serviceable to him in bringing such men in, as I thought had a spirit that would do something in the work. This is very true that I tell you, God knows I lie not. 'Your troops,' said I, 'are most of them old decayed serving men, and tapsters, and such kind of fellows; and,' said I, 'their troops are gentlemen's sons, younger sons, and persons of quality: do you think that the spirits of such base and mean fellows Will ever be enabled to encounter gentleman that have honor, and courage, and resolution in them?' Truly, I presented him in this manner conscientiously; and truly I did tell him, 'You must get men of a spirit: and take it not ill what I say (I know you will not), of a spirit that is likely to go on as far as gentlemen will go, or else I am sure you will be beaten still;' I told him so, I did truly. He was a wise and worthy person, and he did think that I talked a good notion, but an impracticable one. Truly I told him I could do somewhat in it; I did so;

and truly I must needs say that to you, I raised such men as had the fear of God before them, and made some conscience of what they did; and from that day forward, I must say to you, they were never beaten, and wherever they engaged against the enemy, they beat continually."

Acting upon this principle, Cromwell raised a troop of horse among his countrymen, mostly freeholders and freeholders' sons, men thoroughly imbued with his own puritanical opinions, and who engaged in the war "upon matter of conscience:" and thus, says Whitelocke, "being well armed within by the satisfaction of their own consciences, and without by good iron arms, they would as one man stand firmly, and charge desperately."[23] Cromwell knew his men, and on this occasion acting without hypocrisy, tried whether their consciences were proof; for upon raising them he told them fairly that he would not cozen them by perplexed expressions in his commission to fight for king and parliament: if the king chanced to be in the body of the enemy, he would as soon discharge his pistol upon him, as upon any private man; and if their consciences would not let them do the like, he advised them not to enlist themselves under him.

He tried their courage also, as well as their consciences, by leading them into a false ambuscade; about twenty turned their backs and fled; upon which Cromwell dismissed them, desiring them however to leave their horses for those who would fight the Lord's battles in their stead. And as the Lord's battle was to be fought with the arm of flesh, he took special care that horse and man in his troop should always be ready for service; and by making every man trust to himself alone, in all needful things, he enabled them all to rely upon each other, and act with confidence, without which courage is of little avail. For this purpose he required them to keep their arms clean, bright and fit for immediate use; to feed and dress their own horses, and if need were, to sleep upon the ground with them. The officers wishing that this select troop should be formed into what they called 'a gathered church,' looked about for a fitting pastor, and it is to their credit that they pitched upon a man distinguished for his blameless manner of life, his undoubted piety, and his extraordinary talents. They invited Baxter to take charge of them. That remarkable man was then at Coventry, whither he had gone after the battle at Edgehill with a purpose to stay there, as

---

[23] Whitelocke, ed. 1732, p. 72.

a safe place, till one side or other had gotten the victory and the war was ended; "for," says he, "so wise in matters of war was I, and all the country besides, that we commonly supposed that a very few days or weeks, by one other battle, would end the wars; and I believe that no small number of the parliament men had no more wit than to think so." Baxter was at that time so zealous in his political feelings, that he thought it a sin for any man to remain neuter. But the invitation to take charge of 'a gathered church' did not accord with his opinions concerning ecclesiastical discipline. He therefore sent them a denial, reproving their attempt, and telling them wherein his judgment was against the lawfulness and convenience of their way. "These very men," he says, "that then invited me to be their pastor, were the men that afterward headed much of the army, and some of them were the forwardest in all our changes; which made me wish that I had gone among them, however it had been interpreted; for then all the fire was in one spark."

Cromwell exerted himself with so much zeal and success in imbodying and disciplining these troops, that he appears to have been raised to the rank of colonel for that service alone. The first act which he performed was to take possession of Cambridge, which Lord Capel would else have occupied; and to secure for the parliament the college plate, which otherwise would have been sent to the king. At this time he paid his uncle and godfather, Sir Oliver, a visit for the purpose of taking away his arms and all his plate: but behaving with the greatest personal respect to the head of his family, he asked his blessing, and would not keep on his hat in his presence. From Cambridge he kept down the loyal party in the adjoining counties of Suffolk and Norfolk, dispersing a confederacy which would soon have become formidable, and taking the whole of the stores which they had provided. This was a service which, in the language of the saints, was said to set the whole country right, by freeing it of the malignants. Stories of his cruelty were told at this time in the *Mercurius Aulicus* which were abominably false: men too easily believe evil of their enemies; and these calumnies obtained the readier credit, because he and his men conceived themselves to be doing a work of reformation in injuring Peterborough cathredal, demolishing the painted windows, breaking the organ, defacing tombs and statues, and destroying the books. But in other places where the ferocious spirit of puritanism was not called forth, their conduct was more orderly than that of any other troops who were engaged on the same side. One of the journals of the day says of them, "no man swears but he pays his twelvepence; if he be drunk, he is set in stocks, or worse; if one calls the other round-head, he is cashiered; insomuch that the countries where they come leap for joy of them, and come in and join with them. How happy were it if all the forces were thus disciplined!"

The relief of Gainsborough (23d July, 1643) was the first conspicuous action in which Cromwell was engaged: "this," Whitelock says, "was the beginning of his great fortunes, and now he began to appear to the world."[24] It was in this action that Charles Cavendish fell,

> "The young, the lovely, and the brave!
> Strew bays and flowers on his honored grave!"

one of the many noble spirits who were cut off in that mournful war.[25] Cromwell says they had the *execution* of the enemy two or three miles, and that some of his soldiers killed two or three men apiece. He had a narrow escape the same year under the earl of Manchester, when part of Newcastle's army were defeated near Horncastle.[26] His horse was killed under him, and as he rose he was again knocked down, by the cavalier who charged him, and who is supposed to have been Sir Ingram Hopton. He was however remounted, and found himself, with that singular good fortune which always attended him, without a wound. At the close of the year he took Hilsdon house by assault, and alarmed Oxford.[27] Though Essex and Waller, who was called by his own party William the Conqueror, were still the favorite leaders of the parliamentary forces, Cromwell was now looked upon as a considerable person, and was opposed in public opinion to Prince Rupert, before they ever met as hostile generals in the field. When the prince was preparing to relieve York, the London journals represented him as afraid to try himself against this rising commander. "He would rather suffer," they said, "his dear friends in York to perish than venture the loss of his honor in so dangerous a passage. He loves not to meet a Fairfax, nor a Cromwell, nor any of those men that have

---

[24] Whitelock, ed. 1732, p. 72. Whitelock calls him Colonel Cromwell; he served at this time under Lord Willoughby of Parham.

[25] Cousin to the loyal marquis of Newcastle, and brother to the third earl of Devonshire.

[26] Ludlow's Memoirs, ed. 1771, p. 30.

[27] And so went on to Gloucester. Whitelock, p. 82.

so much religion and valor in them." The battle of Marston Moor (2d July, 1644) soon followed; most rashly and unjustifiably brought on by Rupert, without consulting the marquis of Newcastle, by whom, in all prudence, he ought to have been directed, and at a time when nothing but an immediate action could have prevented the Scotch and parliamentary armies from quarrelling and separating, so that either, or both, would have been exposed to an utter overthrow. The Scotch, who were in the right wing, were completely routed; they fled in all directions, and were taken or knocked on the head by the peasantry: their general himself was made prisoner ten miles from the field by a constable. But the fortune of the day was decided by the English horse under Fairfax and Cromwell. They were equal in courage to the king's troops, and superior in discipline: and by their exertions a victory was gained, of which they were left to make full advantage at leisure, owing to the egregious misconduct of the prince, and the resentment of the earl of Newcastle, which in that fatal hour prevailed over a noble mind, and made him forsake the post of duty in disgust.

Hollis in his memoirs has the folly as well as the baseness to accuse Cromwell of cowardice in this action.[28] Some intention of detracting from his deserts seems to have been suspected at the time. The "Mercurius Britannicus" says, "There came out something in print which made a strange relation of the battle: 'tis pity the gallant Cromwell and his godly soldiers are so little heard on, and they with God were so much seen in the battle! But in these great achievements by night, it is hard to say who did most, or who did least. The best way to end our quarrel of who did most, is to say God did all." On the other hand, Cromwell's partisans, to magnify his reputation, gave out that certain troops of horse, picked men, all Irish and all papists, had been appointed by Prince Rupert, to charge in that part where he was stationed. And reports as slanderous as those which charged him with want of courage, were spread abroad to give him the whole credit of the day: it was said that he had stopped the commander-in-chief, Manchester, in the act of flight, saying to him, "You are mistaken, my lord: the enemy is not there!" The earl of Manchester was as brave as Cromwell himself; no man who engaged in the rebellion demeaned himself throughout its course so honorably and so

---

[28] Hollis accuses him of cowardice not only at Marston-Moor, but at Basing-House and Keynton. See Hollis's Life of Himself, in vol. i., of Maseres's tracts.

humanely (Colonel Hutchinson, in his station, perhaps alone excepted), and no man repented more sincerely, nor more frankly avowed his repentance for the part he had taken, when he saw the extent of the misery which he had largely contributed to bring upon his country.

Cromwell was now becoming an object of dislike or jealousy to those leaders of the rebellion whose reputation waned as his increased, or who had insanely supposed, when they let the waters loose, that it would at any time be in their power to restrain them again within their proper bounds. The open declaration which he made against the king at the commencement of hostilities, they had perhaps regarded with complacency, taking credit to themselves for comparative moderation. Because they could manage a party, they fancied themselves capable of managing a rebellion, not remembering, or not knowing, that

> "When evil strives, the worst have greatest names:"

and not perceiving that when Cromwell, in opposition to the impudent hypocrisy of the parliament's language respecting the king, spoke boldly out like one who was resolved to go all lengths, by that declaration he became the head of that party which, in all such convulsions, is sure to obtain the ascendency. From the known opinions of Ireton, and the probable ones of Hampden, the two men whom he seems to have regarded with most deference, it is most likely that he entered into the war as a republican; and now he scrupled not to let his principles be known, saying he hoped soon to see the time when there would not be a single lord in England, and when Lord Manchester would be called nothing more than Mr. Montague. But in his political as in his puritanical professions, Cromwell, who began in sincerity, was now acting a part. Experience was not lost upon so sagacious a man. The more he saw of others, the higher he was led to rate himself; and Hobbes seems to have taken the just view of his motives when he says that his main policy was always to serve the strongest party well, and to proceed as far as that and fortune would carry him.

But Cromwell, who seldom mistook the characters of men, deceived himself when he supposed that he could make Manchester his instrument, as he afterward duped Fairfax. For this must have been his secret object when discoursing with him freely upon the state of the kingdom, and proposing something to which the earl replied that the parliament would never approve it, he made answer, "My lord, if you will stick firm to honest men, you shall find yourself in the head of an army that shall give the law to king and parliament." This startled Manchester, who already knew him to be a man of deep designs: and the manner in which the speech was received made Cromwell perceive that the earl must be set aside, as a person who was altogether unfit for his views. Their mutual dislike broke out after the second battle of Newbury.[29] Cromwell would have attempted to bring that doubtful conflict to a decided issue, by charging the king's army in their retreat; and from the excellent discipline of his brigade, and his skill and intrepidity in action, it is probable he might have inflicted a severe blow upon troops who, it is acknowledged on their own part, were well enough pleased to be rid of an enemy that handled them so ill. But Manchester thought the hazard too great in that season, being the winter, and that the ill consequences of a defeat would be far greater than the advantage to be gained by a victory; for, he said, if they should be routed before Essex's army were reinforced, there would be an end of their pretences; and they should be all rebels and traitors, and executed as such by law. Cromwell repeated this to the house of commons, and accused him of having betrayed the parliament out of cowardice: Manchester justified himself, and in return charged Cromwell with the advice which he had offered him, to overawe both king and parliament by means of the army. This open rapture occasioned much debate and animosity, and much alarm. "What," it was said, "shall we continue bandying one against another? See what a wide gap and door of reproach we open unto the enemy! A plot from Oxford could have done no more than work a distance between our best resolved spirits." The parliament, though indignant at first at what the earl had said concerning the course of law in case of their overthrow, were on the other hand alarmed at the discovery of a danger from their own army, which, if it had been apprehended by far-sighted men, had never before been declared. Inquiry was called for, more on account of Cromwell's designs than the earl's error of judgment; and the independents, as Cromwell's party now began to be called, chose rather to abandon their charge against Manchester, than risk the consequences of further investigation.

---

[29] 27th October, 1644. The first battle was fought 2oth Sept. 1643.

Manchester, on his part, made no further stir,—contented with as much repose as a mind not altogether satisfied with itself would allow him to enjoy. But Essex, the lord-general, who had acted less from mistaken principles than from weakness and vanity and pride, which made him the easy instrument of designing men, gave on this occasion the only instance of political foresight which he ever displayed. He perceived that Cromwell was a dangerous man; and taking council with Hollis and Stapleton, leading men among the presbyterians, and with the Scotch commissioners, resolved, if it were possible, to disable one whose designs were so justly to be apprehended. In serving with the Scotch, Cromwell had contracted some dislike and some contempt for them; which they were not slow in perceiving, as indeed he took little pains to disguise it; and Essex was in hopes that the Scotch might be brought forward to overthrow a man whom he how considered a formidable rival, as by their means the plans for rebellion had first been ripened, and the superiority afterward obtained for the parliamentary forces. A meeting was held at his house to deliberate upon the best mode of proceeding, and Whitelock and Maynard were sent for at a very late hour, to give their opinions as lawyers. The Scotch chancellor explained the business to them in a characteristic speech. He began by assuring "Master Maynard and Master Whitelock" of the great opinion which he and his brethren had of their worth and abilities, else that meeting would not have been desired. "You ken vary weel," said he (as Whitelock reports his words), "that Lieutenant-General Cromwell is no friend of ours; and since the advance of our army into England, he hath used all underhand and cunning means to take off from our honor and merit of this kingdom; an evil requital of all our hazards and services. But so it is; and we are nevertheless fully satisfied of the affections and gratitude of the gude people of this nation in the general. It is thought requisite for us, and for the carrying on the cause of the twa kingdoms, that this obstacle or remora may be removed out of the way, whom, we foresee, will otherwise be no small impediment to us and the gude design we have undertaken. He not only is no friend to us and to the government of our church, but he is also no wellwisher to his excellency, whom you and we all have cause to love and honor: and if he be permitted to go on his ways, it may, I fear, endanger the whole business; therefore we are to advise of some course to be taken for the prevention of that mischief. You ken vary weel the accord twixt the twa kingdoms, and the union by the solemn league and covenant; and if any be an *incendiary* between the twa nations, how he is to be proceeded against. Now the matter is, wherein we desire your opinions, what you tak the meaning of this word *incendiary* to be, and whether Lieutenant-General Cromwell be not sic an *incendiary* as is meant thereby, and whilk way wud be best to tak to proceed against him, if he be proved to be sic an *incendiary*, and that will clip his wings from soaring to the prejudice of our cause. Now you may ken that by our law in Scotland we clepe him an *incendiary* wha kindleth coals of contention, and raises differences in the state to the public damage, and he is *tanquam publicus hostis patriæ*. Whether your law be the same or not, you ken best wha are mickle learned therein: and, therefore, with the favor of his excellency we desire your judgments in these points."[30]

Whitelock and Maynard were men of whom Lord Clarendon, who was intimate with them before the rebellion, has said, that "though they bowed their knees to Baal, and so swerved from their allegiance, it was with less rancor and malice than other men. They never led, but followed, and were rather carried away with the torrent than swam with the stream, and failed through those infirmities which less than a general defection and a prosperous rebellion could never have discovered." Such men were not likely to advise bold measures, in which they might be called upon to bear a part. They admitted the meaning of the word *incendiary* as defined by the Scotch chancellor, and as it stood in the covenant; but they required proofs of particular words or action tending to kindle the fire of contention: they themselves had heard of none, and till the Scotch commissioners could collect such, they were of opinion that the business had better be deferred. And they spoke of the influence and favor which the person in question possessed. "I take Lieutenant-General Cromwell," said Whitelock, "to be a gentleman of quick and subtle parts, and one who hath, especially of late, gained no small interest in the house of commons; nor is he wanting of friends in the house of peers, nor of abilities in himself to manage his own part or defence to the best advantage."[31] Hollis, Stapleton, and some others, related certain acts and sayings of Cromwell which they considered such proofs as the law required, and they were for proceeding boldly with the design. But the Scotch, who, at that time, had less at stake than the leaders of the English presbyterians, chose

---

[30] Whitelock, p. 116, ed. 1732.
[31] Whitelock, p. 117, ed. 1732.

the wary part; and Essex was always incapable of doing either good or evil, except as a tool in the hands of others.

Cromwell was too able a politician not to have agents at all times in the enemy's quarters. Some who were present at this meeting were "false brethren." Whitelock and Maynard were liked by him the better for the opinion they had given; the attack which they had averted might easily have put an end to his career of advancement: a sense of the danger which he had escaped quickened his own measures, and with the co-operation of his friends, and others with whom he then acted, the self-denying ordinance was brought forward, an act which may justly be considered as a masterpiece of his hypocritical policy. To effect this the alarm was first sounded by the "drum ecclesiastic;" the pulpits were manned on one of the appointed fast days, and the topic which the London preachers everywhere insisted on, was the reproach to which parliament was liable for the great emoluments which its members secured to themselves by the civil or military offices which they held; the necessity of removing this reproach, and of praying that God would take his own work into his own hand, and inspire other instruments to perfect what was begun, if those he had already employed were not worthy to bring so glorious a design to a conclusion. Parliament met the next day, and Sir Harry Vane (who, though a thorough fanatic in his notions, could not have acted more hypocritically if he had been pure knave) told them that if ever God had appeared to them, it was in the exercise of yesterday; he was credibly informed that the same lamentations and discourses as the godly preachers had made before them, had been made in all other churches and this could only have proceeded from the immediate spirit of God. He then offered to resign an office which he himself held. Cromwell took up the strain; desired that he might lay down his commission, enlarged upon the vices which were got into the army, "the profaneness and impiety, and absence of all religion, drinking, gaming, and all manner of license and laziness." Till the whole army were new modelled, he said, and governed under a stricter discipline, they must not expect any notable success; and he desired the parliament not to be terrified with an imagination that if the highest offices were vacant, they should not be able to fill them with fit men, for, besides that it was not good to put so much trust in any arm of flesh as to think such a cause depended upon any one man, he took upon himself to assure them they had officers in their army who were fit to be generals in any enterprise in

Christendom. The self-denying ordinance[32] was brought in, and after long debates, and some contests between the two houses, it was carried. Essex was laid aside to reflect at leisure upon the irreparable evils which, through his agency, had been brought upon kingdom, and Sir Thomas Fairfax was appointed general in his stead.

Few men have ever possessed in such perfect as Cromwell the art of rendering others subservient to purposes which they abhorred, and of making individuals of the most opposite characters, views, and principles, co-operate in a design which they would all have opposed if they had perceived it. This rare dissembler availed himself at the same time of the sensual and profligate unbeliever, the austere sectarian, and the fierce enthusiast; and played his master-game at once with Vane and Fairfax, though the former had the craft

---

[32] Mr. Oliver Cromwell endeavors to refute Lord Clarendon's account of the origin of this ordinance. His arguments are, that in Cromwell's speech as given by Rushworth there is no allusion to the fast sermons of the preceding day, and that in fact the fast was not appointed till after the ordinance was past. That this gentleman should on all occasions be desirous of exculpating and vindicating his celebrated ancestor, is to be expected;—there are cases in which erroneous opinions have their root in such good and noble feelings, that he who would eradicate them must profess a sterner philosophy than a good man would willingly adopt. In the present instance it has been overlooked by Mr. Cromwell, that the fast of which he speaks was ordered to implore a blessing on the intended new model of the army, after the ordinance was past; and that that of which Clarendon speaks was appointed to "*seek* God and desire his assistance to lead them out of the perplexities they were in." A punster of that age said that fast days were properly so called because they came so fast—they were frequently three or four in a month. He has also failed to observe that the direct allusion to the preceding fast was made not by Cromwell, but by Sir Harry Vane. And when he censures Lord Clarendon for "taking upon himself to determine the motives of those who brought about that ordinance," he forgets that the same motives are hinted at, not obscurely, by Rushworth, and directly stated by Whitelock, upon the avowal of some of the parties themselves. "Some of them," he says, "confess that this was their design; and it was apparent in itself, and the reason of their doing this was to make way for others, and because they were jealous that the lord-general was too much a favorer of peace, and that he would be too strong a supporter of monarchy and of nobility and other old constitutions, which they had a mind to alter." The only apparent error which Mr. Cromwell has pointed out in Lord Clarendon's statement is his saying that Whitelock voted for the ordinance, Whitelock having inserted in his memorials his speech against that measure. But it is very probable that he who opposed the ordinance in December when it was brought forward, might have assented to it three months afterward for the reason assigned by Clarendon, "that there would be a general dissatisfaction among the people of London if it were rejected."

of the serpent, and the latter the simplicity of the dove, however unlike that bird in other respects. When Fairfax looked back upon his exploits, he rightly accounted them as his greatest misfortunes, and desired no other memorial of them than the act of oblivion: but he well knew that errors like his are not to be forgotten—that they are to be recorded as a warning for others; and the meager memorial which he left of his own actions is not so valuable for anything as for the expression of that feeling, wishing that he had died before he accepted the command after the self-denying ordinance was passed. "By votes of the two houses of parliament," he says, "I was nominated, though most unfit, and so far from desiring it, that had not so great an authority (which was then unseparated from the royal interest) commanded my obedience, and had I not been urged by the persuasion of my nearest friends, I should have refused so great a charge. But whether it was from a natural facility in me that betrayed my modesty, or the powerful hand of God, which all things must obey, I was induced to receive the command—though not fully recovered from a dangerous wound which I had received a little before, and which I believe, without the miraculous hand of God, had proved mortal. But here, alas! when I bring to mind the sad consequences that crafty and designing men have brought to pass since those first innocent undertakings, I am ready to let go that confidence I once had with God, when I could say with Job, 'till I die I will not remove my integrity from me, nor shall my heart reproach me so long as I live.' But I am now more fit to take up his complaint, and say, 'why did I not die?' Why did I not give up the ghost when my life was on the confines of the grave?" Fairfax was a good soldier, but he had no other talents. It is saying little for him that he meant well, seeing he was so easily persuaded not only to permit wicked actions to be done, but to commit them himself. His understanding was so dull, that even in this passage he speaks of the parliament as not being at that time separated from the interests of the king; and his feelings were so obtuse, that even when he penned this memorial he felt no remorse for the execution of Lucas, and Lisle, and the excellent Lord Capel, whose blood was upon his head, but justified what he had done as according to his commission and the trust reposed in him!

Such a man was easily induced to request that the ordinance might be dispensed with in Cromwell's behalf, first for a limited time and then indefinitely, to act under him as commander of the horse. They crippled the royal forces in the west, where so much zeal and heroic virtue had successfully been displayed on the king's side, but where everything now went to ruin under the profligate misconduct of Goring, a general who, notwithstanding his unquestionable courage and military talents, ought to have been considered as disqualified for any trust by his vices. Ere long they were ordered to the north, where Charles had struck a great blow by the taking of Leicester (May, 1645), and where his fortunes might still have been retrieved had it not been for the unsteadiness and irresolution of those about him, and that unhappy diffidence of himself which made him so often act against his own judgment in deference to others.

"With shaking thoughts no hands can draw aright!"

After some injudicious movements, the effect of bad information and vacillating councils, the king met the enemy at Naseby (14th June, 1645). All those accidents upon which so much depends in war were against him; his erroneous information continued till the very hour of the action, so that the good order in which his army had been drawn up was broken, and the advantageous position which they had occupied abandoned; in the action itself the same kind of misconduct, which had proved so disastrous at Marston Moor, was committed, with consequences still more fatal. Prince Rupert in time of action always forgot the duty of a general, suffering himself to be carried away by mere animal courage; no experience, however dearly brought, was sufficient to cure him of this fault. His charge, as usual, was irresistible; but having broken and routed that wing of the enemy which was opposed to him, he pursued them as if the victory were secure. In this charge Ireton was wounded, thrown from his horse, and taken. The day was won by Cromwell, whose name is not mentioned by Ludlow in his account of the battle![33] An unaccountable incident contributed to, and perhaps mainly occasioned its loss. Just as the king, at the head of his reserve, was about to charge Cromwell's horse, the earl of Carnewarth suddenly seized his bridle, exclaiming, with or three full-mouthed Scottish oaths, "Will you go upon your death in an instant?"[34] A cry ran through the troops that they should march to the right,

---

[33] Ludlow's Memoirs, p. 65, ed. 1771.
[34] Clar. Hist., vol. v., p. 185, ed. 1826.

in which direction the king's horse had been turned, and which, in the situation of the field, was bidding them shift for themselves. It was in vain that Charles, with great personal exertion and risk, endeavored to rally them. Neither these troops nor Prince Rupert's, when he returned from his rash pursuit, could be brought to rally and form in order; a most important part of discipline, in which the soldiers under Fairfax and Cromwell were perfect, the latter having now modelled the army as he had from the beginning his own troop. The day was irrecoverably lost, and with it the king and the kingdom. The number of slain on the king's part did not exceed 700, but more than 5,000 prisoners were taken, being the whole of the infantry, with all the artillery and baggage. In the pursuit above a hundred women were killed (such was the temper of the conquerors!) some of whom were the wives of officers of quality. The king's cabinet fell into their hands, with the letters between him and the queen, "of which," says Clarendon, "they made that barbarous use as was agreeable to their natures, and published them in print; that is, so much of them as they thought would asperse either of their majesties, and improve the prejudice they had raised against them; and concealed other parts which would have vindicated them from many particulars with them which they had aspersed them."[35]

Upon this act of the parliament the king has expressed his feelings in the Icon in that calm strain of dignity by which the book is distinguished and authenticated. "The taking of my letters," he says, "was an opportunity which, as the malice of mine enemies could hardly have expected, so they knew not how with honor and civility to use it. Nor do I think, with sober and worthy minds, anything in them could tend so much to my reproach as the odious divulging of them did to the infamy of the divulgers: the greatest experiments of virtue and nobleness being discovered in the greatest advantages against an enemy; and the greatest obligations being those which are put upon us by them from whom we could least have expected them. And such I should have esteemed the concealing of my papers, the freedom and secresy of which command a civility from all men not wholly barbarous. Yet since Providence will have it so, I am content so much of my heart (which I study to approve to God's omniscience) should be discovered to the world, without any of those

---

[35] Clar. Hist., vol. v., p. 186, ed. 1826.

dresses or popular captations which some men use in their speeches and expresses. I wish my subjects had yet a clearer sight into my most retired thoughts; where they might discover how they are divided between the love and care I have, not more to preserve my own rights than to preserve their peace and happiness; and that extreme grief to see them both deceived and destroyed. Nor can any men's malice be gratified farther by my letters than to see my constancy to my wife, the laws, and religion." Then speaking of his enemies, he says "They think no victories so effectual to their designs as those that most rout and waste my credit with my people; in whose hearts they seek by all means to smother and extinguish all sparks of love, respect, and loyalty to me, that they may never kindle again, so as to recover mine, the law's and the kingdom's liberties, which some men seek to overthrow. The taking away of my credit, is but a necessary preparation to the taking away of my life and my kingdom. First I must seem neither fit to live, nor worthy to reign. By exquisite methods of cunning and cruelty, I must be compelled first to follow the funerals of my honor, and then be destroyed."

In another of these beautiful meditations, looking back upon the course of the war, he says "I never had any victory which was without my sorrow, because it was on mine own subjects, who, like Absalom, died many of them in their sin. And yet I never suffered any defeat which made me despair of God's mercy and defence. I never desired such victories as might serve to conquer, but only restore the laws and liberties of my people, which I saw were extremely oppressed, together with my rights, by those men who were impatient of any just restraint. When Providence gave me or denied me victory, my desire was neither to boast of my power nor to charge God foolishly, who I believed at last would make all things to work together for my good. I wished no greater advantages by the war than to bring my enemies to moderation and my friends to peace. I was afraid of the temptation of an absolute conquest, and never prayed more for victory over others than over myself. When the first was denied, the second was granted me, which God saw best for me."

The influence of pure religion upon a sound understanding and a gentle heart has never been more finely exemplified than by Charles during the long course of his afflictions. Cromwell also was religious, but his religion at the time when it was most sincere was most alloyed, and it acted upon an intellect and disposition most unlike the king's. Clear as his head was in action, his apprehension ready, and his mind comprehensive as well as firm; when out of the sphere of business and command, his notions were confused and muddy, and his language stifled the thoughts it affected to bring forth; producing, by its curious infelicity, a more than oracular obscurity. The letter which he addressed to the speaker after the battle of Naseby is one of the most lucid specimens of his misty style. After saying that for three hours the fight had been very doubtful, and stating what were the results of the action, he proceeds thus: "Sir, this is none other but hand of God, and to him alone belongs the glory, wherein none are to share with him. The general has served you with all faithfulness and honor; and the best commendation I can give him is, that I dare say he attributes all to God, and would rather perish than assume to himself, which is an honest and a thriving way; and yet as much for bravery may be given to him in this action, as to a man. Honest men served you faithfully in this action. Sir, they are trusty. I beseech you in the name of God not to discourage them. I wish this action may beget thankfulness and humility in all that are concerned in it. He that ventures his life for the liberty of his country, I wish he trust God for the liberty of his conscience, and you for the liberty he fights for. In this he rests who is your most humble servant, OLIVER CROMWELL."[36]

After the fatal defeat at Naseby (June 14, 1645), the royal cause soon became hopeless. Bristol was not better defended by Prince Rupert than it had been by Nathaniel Fiennes. During the siege, Fairfax and Cromwell narrowly escaped from being killed by the same ball. The latter declared none but an atheist could deny that their success was the work of the Lord. In his official letter he said, "It may be thought some praises are due to these gallant men of whose valor so much mention is made; their humble suit to you and all that have an interest in this blessing, is, that in remembrance of God's praises they may be forgotten. It's their joy that they are instruments to God's glory and their country's good. It's their honor that God vouchsafes to use them. Sir, they that have been employed in this service know that faith and prayer obtained this city for you." The faith and prayers of William Dell and Hugh Peters, chaplains to the besieging forces, were assisted by the experience of Skippon in military operations, by the fear of a disaffected party within the

---

[36] Ellis's Letters, vol. iii., p. 305, first series.

city, and by the sample which the besiegers had given of their intention to put their enemies to the sword if they took the place by storm. Cromwell next took Devizes (September, 1645), and disarmed and dispersed the clubmen in Hampshire, who having originally associated to protect themselves against the excesses of both parties, contributed to the miseries of the country by making a third party as oppressive as either. Winchester surrendered to him (October 5, 1645), and on that occasion he gave an honorable example of fidelity to his engagements: six of his men being detected in plundering, in violation of the terms of capitulation, he hung one of them,[37] and sent the other five to the king's governor at Oxford, to be punished at his discretion. Basing House, which had been so long and bravely defended, yielded (Tuesday, October 14, 1645) to this fortunate general, who never failed in any enterprise which he undertook. He then rejoined Fairfax in the west, to complete the destruction of a gallant army which had been ruined by worthless and wicked commanders. Lord Hopton, one of those men whose virtues redeem the age, had taken the command of it in a manner more honorable to himself than the most glorious of those achievements in which he had formerly been successful: there was no possibility of averting or even delaying a total defeat. When Prince Charles entreated him to take upon himself the forlorn charge of commanding it, Lord Hopton replied that it was the custom now, when men were not willing to submit to what they were enjoined, to say it was against their honor: for himself he could not obey in this instance without resolving to lose his honor: but since his highness thought it necessary so to command him, even at that cost he was ready to obey. He made so gallant a resistance at Torrington,[38] though great part of his men behaved basely, that the parliamentary forces suffered greater loss than at any other storm in which they were engaged; and when his army was finally broken up, as much by the license and mutinous temper of the men and officers, as by the enemy's overpowering force, he disdained to make terms for himself, and retired with the ammunition, and those who remained faithful, into Pendennis castle. The last possibility which remained to the king of collecting an army in the field was destroyed when Lord Astley was defeated by superior numbers and

---

[37] They first cast lots for their lives. Rushworth, fol. 1701, p. 92.
[38] Against Fairfax, February, 1645-'46.

taken.[39] At the beginning of the war, this gallant soldier, before he charged in the battle of Edgehill, made a prayer, of which Hume says, there were certainly much longer ones said in the parliamentary army, but it may be doubted whether there were so good a one. It was simply this: "O Lord! thou knowest how busy I must be this day! If I forget thee, do not thou forget me." He now concluded his brave and irreproachable career, by a saying not less to be remembered by the enemy's officers: "You have done your work, and may now go to play, unless you choose to fall out among yourselves."

Even before the loss of Bristol,[40] Charles, whose judgment seldom deceived him, had seen that the worst was to be expected, and made up his mind to endure it as became him. In reply to a letter from Prince Rupert, who had advised him again to propose a treaty after that at Uxbridge had failed, he pointed out the certainty that no terms would be granted which it would not be criminal in him to accept; and at the same time fairly acknowledged the hopelessness of his affairs, save only for his trust in God. "I confess," he said, "that speaking either as to mere soldier or statesman, I must say there is no probability but of my ruin: but as to Christian, I must tell you that God will not suffer rebels to prosper, or his cause to be overthrown: and whatsoever personal punishment it shall please him to inflict upon me, must not make me repine, much less to give over the quarrel. Indeed, I can not flatter myself with expectation of good success more than this, to end my days with honor and a good conscience; which obliges me to continue my endeavors, as not despairing that God may in due time avenge his own cause. Though I must avow to all my friends that he that will stay with me at this time must expect and resolve, either to die for a good cause, or, which is worse, to live as miserable in the maintaining it, as the violence of insulting rebels can make him." The prospect of dying in the field, which it appears from these expressions the king contemplated with a complacent resignation, and perhaps with hope, was at an end when Lord Astley was defeated: in expectation of this he had already consulted for the safety of the prince of Wales, and it was now to be determined whither he should betake himself. He offered to put himself in the hands of two commanders who at some distance were blockading Oxford, if they would pass their words that they would

---

[39] Near Stow in the Wold in Gloucestershire, 21st March, 1645-'46.
[40] Prince Rupert surrendered Bristol to Sir Thomas Fairfax, 11th September, 1645.

immediately conduct him to the parliament; for in battle or in debate Charles was always ready to face his enemies, and in debate with the advantage of a collected mind, a sound judgment, a ready utterance, and a thorough knowledge of the points in dispute. He knew also that, throughout this fatal contest, the hearts of a great majority of the people were with him; and though the strength of the rebellious party lay in London, yet even there he thought so much loyalty was left, and so much regard for his person, that he would willingly have been in it at this time. But the parliamentary generals, whose purpose it always was to prevent the possibility of any accommodation which would have restored even a nominal authority to the sovereign, refused to enter into any such engagement; and the avenues of the city were strictly watched, lest he should enter secretly. Another and better hope was to join Montrose, who was then in his career of victory. The representations of M. Montrevil, a French agent, who was at that time with the Scotch army before Newark, and the promises of the Scotch made to that agent, that they would receive him as their sovereign, and effectually join with him for the recovery of his just rights, induced him to take that step. "They have often," he says, "professed they have fought against me, but for me. I must now resolve the riddle of their loyalty, and give them opportunity to let the world see they mean not what they do, but what they say."

When that memorable bargain was concluded, by which the Scotch sold and the English bought their king, Cromwell was one of the commissioners. Yet it is represented by his bitterest enemy, Hollis, that nothing could have been so desirable for Cromwell, and nothing could have been so desirable from Cromwell, and nothing so much wished for by that party who were bent upon destroying monarchy, as that the Scotch should have taken Charles with them into Scotland, instead of delivering him into the hands of the parliament; and he speaks of the sale as singularly honorable to both the contracting parties! "Here, then," he says, "the very mouth of iniquity was stopped: malice itself had nothing to say to give the least blemish to the faithfulness and reality of the kingdom of Scotland, the clearness of their proceedings, their zeal for peace, without self-seeking and self-ends, or any endeavors to make advantage of the miseries and misfortunes of England."[41]

---

[41] Hollis, in Maseras' tracts, vol. i., p. 230.

Charles himself saw the transaction in a very different light, as posterity has done. He declared that he was bought and sold. "Yet," he says in the Icon, "may I justify those Scots to all the world in this, that they have not deceived me, for I never trusted to them, further than to men. If I am sold by them, I am only sorry they should do it; and that my price should be so much above my Savior's!—Better others betray me than myself, and that the price of my liberty should be my conscience. The greatest injuries my enemies seek to inflict upon me can not be without my own consent."

The Scotch nation in general were sensible of the infamy which had been brought upon them by this act. The English were at first deceived by it: for, rightly perceiving that peace and tranquility could not be restored by any other means than by the restoration of the king to those just rights and privileges which he holds for the good of all, they believed that he was now to be brought in honor and safety to London. As he was taken Newcastle to Holmby, they flocked from all parts to see him; and scrofulous patients were brought to receive the royal touch, in full belief of its virtue, and with entire affection to his person. If the intentions of Hollis and the presbyterian party had been such as they were afterward desirous to make the world believe, they had it in their power now to have imposed upon the king any terms to which he could conscientiously have submitted; and the army were not yet so completely lords of the ascendant as to have prevented such an accommodation. But that party had brought on the civil war; had slandered the king in the foulest spirit of calumny; and on every occasion had acted toward him precisely in that manner which would wound and insult him most: it is impossible to know what catastrophe they designed for the tragedy which they had planned and carried on thus far; but it is not possible that they intended a termination which should have been compatible with the honor and well-being of the sovereign whom they had so bitterly injured. With that brutality which characterized all their proceedings toward him, they refused to let any of his chaplains attend him at this time. There is no subject upon which the king, in his lonely meditations, has expressed himself with more feeling than upon this. He says, "When Providence was pleased to deprive me of all other civil comforts and secular attendants, I thought the absence of them all might best be supplied by the attendance of some of my chaplains, whom for their functions I reverence, and for their fidelity I have cause to love.

By their learning, piety, and prayers, I hoped to be either better enabled to sustain the want of all other enjoyments, or better fitted for the recovery and use of them in God's good time. The solitude they have confined me unto adds the wilderness to my temptation; for the company they obtrude upon me is more sad than any solitude can be. If I had asked my revenues, my power of the militia, or any one of my kingdoms, it had been no wonder to have been denied in those things, where the evil policy of men forbids all just restitution, lest they should confess an injurious usurpation: but to deny me the ghostly comfort of my chaplains seems a greater rigor and barbarity than is ever used by Christians to the meanest prisoners and greatest malefactors. But my agony must not be relieved with the presence of any one good angel; for such I account a learned, godly, and discreet divine: and such I would have all mine to be. To thee, therefore, O God, do I direct my now solitary prayers! What I want of others' help, supply with the more immediate assistance of thy Spirit: in thee is all fulness: from thee is all sufficiency: by thee is all acceptance. Thou art company enough, and comfort enough. Thou art my King, be also my prophet and my priest. Rule me, teach me, pray in me, for me, and be thou ever with me."

The parliamentary leaders had no sooner won the victory than they began to divide the spoils. The parliament, by virtue of that sovereign authority which it had usurped, created Essex and Warwick dukes; Hollis was made a Viscount; Hazlerigg, Vane, Fairfax, and Cromwell, barons, the latter with a revenue of 2,500*l.*, charged upon the estates of the marquis of Worcester. They filled up the places of those members who followed the king's party, or whom their violent measures had driven from the house; and this was done with a contempt of the laws which indicated that the people of England were now under the dominion of the sword. "First," says Hollis (who, being now on the weaker side, could see the enormity of their proceedings),—"first they did all they could to stop writs from going any whither but where they were sure to have fit men chosen for their turns; and many an unjust thing was done by them in that kind; sometimes denying writs, sometimes delaying till they had prepared all things and made it, as they thought, cock sure; many times committee-men in the country, such as were their creatures, appearing grossly, and bandying to carry elections for them; sometimes they did it fairly by the power of the army, causing soldiers to be sent and quartered in the towns where elections were to be; awing and terrifying, sometimes abusing and offering violence to the electors." The self-denying ordinance was totally disregarded now: it had effected the object for which it was designed; and perhaps as the war in England was at an end, it may have been fairly supposed to have expired. Many officers therefore were not returned, and among them, Ludlow, Ireton, and Fairfax. The two former were republicans, who emulated the old Romans in the severity of their character, and looked upon it as a virtue to be inexorable. Ludlow has related of himself that, meeting in a skirmish with an old acquaintance and schoolfellow who was on the king's side, he expressed his sorrow at seeing him in that party, and offered to exchange a shot with him. He relates also that when he was defending Warder Castle, one of the besiegers who was killed, said just before he expired, that he saw his own brother fire the musket by which he received his mortal wound; and instead of expressing a human feeling at his frightful example of the horrors of civil war, he adds that it might probably be, his brother having been one of those who defended the breach where he was shot; "but if it were so, he might justly do it by the laws of God and man, it being done in the discharge of his duty and in his own defence." With such deliberate inhumanity did Ludlow in old age and retirement comment upon a fact, which, even in the fever of political enthusiasm and the heat of battle, ought to have made him shudder.

That party, who would have been satisfied with the establishment of a presbyterian church, and the enjoyment of offices, honors, and emoluments, under a king whom they wished to preserve only as a puppet for their own purposes, would now gladly have reduced an army of which they began to stand in fear: for since it had been new-model-led, the independents had obtained the ascendency there; and those principles which Cromwell at the first avowed to his own troop, were now becoming common among the soldiers. They had been taught to believe that the king was an enemy and a tyrant: and drawing from false premises a just conclusion, they reasoned that, because it was lawful to fight against him, it was right also to destroy him. They saw through the hypocrisy of the presbyterians, whom they called with sarcastic truth the *dissembly* men; and being led by their own situation to speculate upon the origin of dignities and powers, they asked what were the lords of England but William the Conqueror's colonels? or the barons but his majors? or the knights but his captains? The parliament had just reason to fear an army in this temper; and the army had equal reason to complain of the parliament, because their pay was in arrears: they were therefore to be disbanded, the commissioned officers to receive debentures for what was due to them, and the non-commissioned officers and privates a promise, secured upon the excise. But men who had arms in their hands were easily persuaded that they might use them with as much justice to intimidate the parliament, as to subdue the king. That they might have their deliberative assemblies also, under whose authority they might proceed, they appointed a certain number of officers which they called the general council of officers, who were to act as their house of peers; and the common soldiers chose three or four from every regiment, mostly corporals or sergeants, few or none above the rank of an ensign, who were called agitators, and were to be the army's house of commons. The president of these agitators was a remarkable man, by name James Berry; he had originally been a clerk in some iron-works. In the course of the revolution he sat in the upper house. He was one of the principle actors in pulling down Richard Cromwell; became afterward one of the council of state; was imprisoned after the restoration as one of the four men whom Monk considered the most dangerous; and finally, being liberated, became a gardener, and finished his life in obscurity and peace.

Both the council of officers and the agitators were composed of Cromwell's creatures, or of men who, being thorough fanatics, did his work equally well in stupid sincerity. They presented a bold address to parliament declaring that they would neither be divided nor disbanded till their full arrears were paid, and demanding that no member of the army should be tried by any other judicatory than a council of war. "They did not," they said, "look upon themselves as a band of janizaries, hired only to fight the battles of the parliament; they had voluntarily taken up arms for the liberty of the nation of which they were a part, and before they laid those arms down they would see that end well provided for." The men who presented this address behaved with such audacity at the bar of the house of commons, that there were some who moved for their committal: but they had friends even there to protect them, one of whom replied that he would have them committed indeed, but it should be to the best inn in the town, where plenty of good sack and sugar should be provided for them. As the dispute proceeded, the army held louder language, and the parliament took stronger measures, causing some of the boldest among the soldiers to be imprisoned. Cromwell supported the house in this, expressed great indignation at the insolence of the troops, and complained even with tears, that there even been a design of killing him, so odious had he been made to the army by men who were desirous of again imbruing the nation in blood! Yet he had said to Ludlow that "it was a miserable thing to serve a parliament, to whom let a man he never so faithful, if one pragmatical fellow among them rise up and asperse him, he shall never wipe it off; whereas," said he, "when one serves under a general, he may do as much service and yet be free from all blame and envy." And during these very discussions he whispered in the house to Ludlow, "These men will never leave till the army pull them out by the ears." If Ludlow suspected any sinister view in Cromwell, he was himself too much engaged with the army to notice it at that time. But there were other members whose opposite interest opened their eyes; and who, knowing that Cromwell was the secret director of those very measures against which he inveighed, resolved to send him to the tower, believing that if he were once removed, the army might easily be reduced to obedience. They estimated his authority more justly than they did their own. It appears that he expected a more violent contest than actually ensued; for he and many of the independents privately removed their effects from London, "leaving," says Hollis, "city and parliament as marked out for destruction." He had timely notice of the design against him, and on the very morning when they proposed to arrest him, he set out for the army: but still preserving that dissimulation which he never laid aside where it could possibly be useful, he wrote to the house of commons, saying, that his presence was necessary to reclaim the soldiers, who had been abused by misinformation; and desiring that the general (Fairfax), and such other officers who were in the house or in town, might be sent to their quarters to assist him in that good work.

On the very day that Cromwell joined the army, the king was carried from Holmby by Joyce (3d June, 1647). That *gray discrowned head*, as he himself beautifully calls it, the sight of which drew tears from his friends, and moved many even of his enemies to compunction as well as pity, excited no feeling or respect in this hard and vulgar ruffian, who had formerly been a tailor and afterward a menial servant in Hollis's family. He produced a pistol as the authority which the king was to obey, and Charles believed that the intention in carrying him away was to murder him. Whether Joyce was employed by the agitators, of whose body he was one, or whether, as Hollis[42] asserts and as is generally believed, Cromwell sent him, is of no consequence in Cromwell's character (though his descendant strenuously endeavors to show that he had no concern in the transaction), for it is only a question whether he was mediately or immediately the author. The insolence with which the act was performed is imputable to the agent; and there is some reason to believe that, whatever may have been the intention of Ireton, St. John, Vane, and other men of that stamp, Cromwell himself was at that time very far from having determined upon the death of the king. It was plain that the parliament had no intention of making any terms with the king, except such as would have left him less real power than the oligarchs of Venice intrusted to their doge; and it was not less obvious that, as Charles might expect more equitable conditions from the army, who would treat with him as a part of the nation, not as a body contending for sovereignty, so on his side he would come to the treaty with better hope and a kindlier disposition. Indeed, at this time he looked upon them with the feelings of a British king. "Though they have fought against me," said he, "yet I can not but so far esteem that valor and gallantry they have sometimes showed, as to wish I may never want such men to maintain myself, my laws, and my kingdom, in such a peace as wherein they may enjoy their share and proportion as much as any men." He had changed his keepers and his prison, but not his captive condition; only there was this hope of bettering, that they who were such professed patrons of the people's liberty, could not be utterly against the liberty of the king. "What they demanded for their own conscience," said he, "they can not in reason deny to mine;" and it consoled him to believe that the world would now see a king could not be so low as not to be considerable, adding right to that party where he appeared.

So far he was right; it is the lively expression of Hollis that the army made that use of the king which the Philistines would have made of the ark, and that and their power together made them prevail. The description which he gives of the parliament at this crisis holds forth an awful warning to those who fancy that it is as easy to direct the commotions of a state as to excite them; it is a faithful picture drawn by a leading member of that faction which had raised

---

[42] Hollis, in Maseres' tracts, vol. i., p. 246.

and hitherto guided the rebellion: "They now thunder upon us," he says, "with remonstrances, declarations, letters, and messages every day, commanding one day one thing, the next day another, making us vote and unvote, do and undo; and when they had made us do some ugly thing, jeer us, and say our doing justifies their desiring it."[43]—"We feel as low as dirt," he says; "take all our ordinances in pieces, change and alter them according to their minds, and (which is worst of all) expunge our declaration against their mutinous petition, cry *peccavimus* to save a whipping: but all would not do!—All was dashed" (it is still Hollis the parliamentarian who speaks): "instead of a generous resistance to the insolencies of perfidious servants, vindicating the honor of the parliament, discharging the trust that lay upon them to preserve a poor people from being ruined and enslaved to a rebellious army, they deliver up themselves and kingdom to the will of their enemies; prostitute all to the lust of heady and violent men; and suffer Mr. Cromwell to saddle, ride, switch, and spur them at his pleasure." Ride them indeed he did with a martingale; and it was not all the wincing of the galled jade that could shake the practised horseman in his seat. Poor Hollis complains that "presbyterians were trumps no longer." Clubs were trumps now, and the knave in that suit, as in the former, was the best card in the pack. When the parliament had done whatever the army required, "prostituting their honors, renouncing whatever would be of strength or safety to them, casting themselves down naked, helpless, and hopeless, at the proud feet of their domineering masters, it is all to no purpose; it does but encourage those merciless men to trample the more upon them."

So it was, and properly so. This was the reward of the presbyterian party for

> "For letting rapine loose and murther
> To rage just so far and no further,
> And setting all the land on fire
> To burn to a scantling and no higher;
> For venturing to assassinate,
> And cut the throats of church and state."

---

[43] Hollis, in Maseres' tracts, vol. i., p. 254.

This they had done; and instead of being, as they had calculated upon being,

> "Allowed the fittest men
> To take the charge of both again,"

they were now

> "Out-gifted, out-impulsed, outdone,
> And out-revealed at carryings-on;
> Of all their dispensations wormed.
> Out-providenced, and out-reformed,
> Ejected out of church and state,
> And all things—but the people's hate."

As the question stood between the parliament and the army, the army was in the right. Whatever arguments held good for resisting the king, availed *à fortiori* for resisting the parliament; its little finger was heavier than his loins and where the old authorities had used a whip, the parliament had scourged the nation with scorpions. The change in ecclesiastical affairs was of the same kind. New presbyter was old priest written large—and in blacker characters. Cromwell had force of reason as well as force of arms on his side; and if he had possessed a legitimate weight in the country, like Essex, it is likely that he would now have used it to the best purpose, and have done honorably for himself and beneficially for the kingdom, what was afterward effected by Monk, with too little regard to any interest except his own. It is said that he required for himself, as the reward of this service to his sovereign, the garter, the title of the earl of Essex, vacant by the death of the late general (September 14, 1646), and a proper object of ambition to Cromwell, as having formerly been in his family; to be made first captain of the guards, and vicar-general of the kingdom. All this he would have deserved, if he had restored peace and security to the nation by re-establishing the monarchy with those just limitations, the propriety of which was seen and acknowledged by the king himself. But if Cromwell desired to do this, which may reasonably be presumed, the power which he then possessed was not sufficient for it. It was a revolutionary power, not transferable to the better cause without great diminution. In the movements of the revolutionary sphere his star was rising, but it was not yet lord of the ascendant; and in raising himself to his present station, he had, like the unlucky magician in romance, conjured up stronger spirits than he was yet master enough of the black art to control. Under his management, the moral discipline of the army was as perfect as that of the Swedes under the great Gustavus, whom it is not improbable that Cromwell in this point took for his model. He had been most strict and severe in chastising all irregularities, "insomuch," says Clarendon, "that sure there was never any such body of men, so without rapine, swearing, drinking, or any other debauchery—but the wickedness of their hearts." He had brought them to this state by means of religious enthusiasm, the most powerful and the most perilous of all principles which an ambitious man can call into action. When the parliamentary army first took the field, every regiment had its preacher, who beat the drum ecclesiastic, and detorted scripture to serve the purposes of rebellion. The battle of Edgehill (October 23, 1642) sickened them of service in the field; almost all of them went home after that action: and when the tide of success set in against the king, they had little inclination to return to their posts, because the other sectaries with whom the army swarmed beat them at their own weapons. Baxter says it was the ministers that lost all, by forsaking the army and betaking themselves to an easier and quieter way of life; and he especially repented that he had not accepted the chaplainship of that famous troop with which Cromwell began his army; persuading himself that if he had been among them, he might have prevented the spreading of that fire which was then in one spark. Baxter is one of those men whose lives exemplify the strength and the weakness of the human mind. He fancied that the bellows which had been used for kindling the fire, could blow it out when the house was in flames! He might as well have supposed that he could put out Etna with an extinguisher, or have stilled an earthquake by setting his foot upon the ground.

In the anarchy which the war produced, some of the preachers acted as officers; and, on the other hand, officers, with at least as much propriety, acted as preachers. Cromwell himself edified the army by his discourses; and every common soldier who carried a voluble tongue, and either was or pretended to be a fanatic, held forth from a pulpit or a tub. The land was overrun with—

> "a various rout
> Of petulant capricious sects,
> The maggots of corrupted texts"—

but they bred in the army; and this license of things spiritual led by a sure process to the wildest notions of political liberty, to which also the constitution of the army was favorable: a mercenary army, Hollis calls it, "all of them, from the general (except what he may have in expectation after his father's death) to the meanest sentinel, not able to make a thousand pounds a year lands, most of the colonels and officers, mean tradesmen, brewers, tailors, goldsmiths, shoemakers, and the like—a notable dunghill, if one would rake into it to find out their several pedigrees." According to him, these "bloodsuckers had conceived a mortal hatred" against his party, "and, in truth, against all gentlemen, as those who had too great an interest and too large a stake of their own in the kingdom, to engage with them in their design of perpetuating the war to an absolute confusion." It was by such instruments that Cromwell had made himself, ostensibly the second person in the army, really the first: but he was not yet their master, and was compelled to court them still by professing a fellowship in opinions which he had ceased to hold. Had he espoused the king's cause heartily and honestly, which probably he desired to do, the very men upon whom his power rested would have turned against him, and have pursued him with as murderous a hatred as that which Pym had avowed against Strafford, and had gratified in his blood. Both in and out of army he needed the co-operation of men some of whom were his equals in cunning, others in audacity: Vans and perhaps St. John were as crafty; Ludlow, Hazlerigg, and many others, were as bold. But these men were bent upon trying the experiment of a republic, to which the king's destruction was a necessary prelude. And he who afterward controlled three nations, is said himself to have stood in some awe of his son-in-law Ireton, a man of great talents and inflexible character, and sincere in those political opinions which Cromwell held only while they were instrumental to his advancement.

Ludlow, who knew Ireton well, and was the more likely to understand the motives of his conduct, because he entirely coincided with him in his political desires, believed that it was never his intention to come to any agreement with the king, but only to delude the loyalists while the army were contesting with the presbyterian interest in parliament: and he relates that Ireton once said to the king, "Sir, you have an intention to be arbitrator between the parliament and us, and we mean to be so between you and the parliament." Cromwell, on the other hand, is said to have declared that the interview between Charles and his children, when they were first allowed to visit him, was "the tenderest sight that ever his eyes beheld;" to have wept plentifully when he spoke of it (which he might well have done without hypocrisy, for in private life he was a man of kind feelings and of a generous nature); to have confessed that "never man was so abused as he in his sinister opinion of the king, who, he thought, was the most upright and conscientious of his kingdom;" and to have imprecated that "God would be pleased to look upon him according to the sincerity of his heart toward the king." There are men so habitually insincere that they seem to delight in acts of gratuitous duplicity, as if their vanity was gratified by the easy triumph over those who are too upright to suspect deceit. Cromwell was a hypocrite, then, only when hypocrisy was useful; there are anecdotes enough which prove that he was well pleased when he could lay aside the mask. In his conduct toward Charles, while that poor persecuted king was with the army, there is no reason to suspect him of any sinister intention; the most probable solution is that also which is most creditable to him, and which is imputed to him by those persons who aspersed him most. Hollis and Ludlow, who hated him with as much inveteracy as if they had not equally hated each other, agree in believing that he would willingly have taken part with the king; and that he was deterred from this better course by the fear that the army would desert him. They agree also that when he was certain of this, he, by taking measures for alarming the king, instigated him to make his escape from Hampton Court (November 11, 1647). Concerning his further[44] purpose, there are different opinions. Hollis, who would allow him no merit, supposes that he directed him to Carisbrook because he knew that Hammond might be depended upon as a jailer: Ludlow supposes that he thought Hammond a man on whom the king might rely; and Hobbes, with more probability than either, affirms that he meant to let him escape from the kingdom, which, with common prudence on the part of his companions, he

---

[44] One of the very few errors which M. Villemain has committed is that of saying that Ashburnham is charged by Clarendon with having betrayed his master on this occasion; whereas Clarendon, though he perceived with what fatal and unaccountable mismanagement they proceeded, entirely acquits him of any intention to mislead the king. M. Villemain writes New York for Newark—from a mistaken etymology, we suppose. These trifling mistakes are pointed out for correction, not from the desire of detecting faults, but in respect for a work of great sagacity, perfect candor, and exemplary diligence—being by far the most able history of Cromwell that has yet been written.

might have done, and which, when Cromwell had made his choice to act with the commonwealth's-men, would have served their purpose better than his death.

He did not, however, join them hastily, not from his own feelings, but as if yielding, rather than consenting, to circumstances. Conferences were held between some of the heads of the many-headed anarchy—members, officers, and preachers—to determine what form of government was best for the nation, whether monarchical, aristocratical, or democratical. The ablest leaders of the presbyterian party had been expelled the house, and some of them driven into exile by the preponderating influence of the army, who availed themselves of the king's presence to obtain that object. These persons, more from their hatred of the independents than from any other principle, would have defended the monarchy, which was now but weakly and insincerely defended by Cromwell and those who were called the grandees of the house and army. Either form of government, they said, might be good in itself, and for them, as Providence should direct; this being interpreted meant that they were ready to support any form which might be most advantageous to themselves. On the other hand, the political and religious zealots insisted that monarchy was in itself an evil, and that the Jews had committed a great sin against the Lord in choosing it; and they, apparently now for the first time, avowed their desire of putting the king to death and establishing an equal commonwealth. Cromwell, who was then acknowledged as the head of the grandees, professed himself to be unresolved; he had learned however the temper of his tools, and with that coarse levity which is one of the strongest features in his character, he concluded the conference by flinging a cushion at Ludlow's head, and then running down stairs; but not fast enough to escape a similar missile which was sent after him. The next day he told Ludlow he was convinced of the desirableness of what that party had proposed, but not of its feasibleness. The time was now fast approaching when Cromwell could find everything feasible which he desired. A bold accusation was preferred against him in the house of lords by Major Huntington: he affirmed that Cromwell and Ireton had, from the beginning, instigated the army to disobey and resist the parliament; that they had pledged themselves to make the king the most glorious prince in Christendom, while they were making use of him, and had declared that they were ready to join with French, Spaniards, Cavaliers, or any who would force the parliament to agree with him; that their real object was to perpetuate the power of the army; that Ireton said, when the king and parliament were treating, he hoped they would make such a peace that the army might, with a good conscience, fight against them both; and that Cromwell had, both in public and private, maintained as his principle that every individual was judge of just and right as to the good and ill of a kingdom; that it was lawful to pass through any forms of government for attaining his end, and that it was lawful to play the knave with a knave. Huntington swore to the truth of these allegations; Milton impugns his credit, by saying that he afterward besought Cromwell's pardon, and confessed that he had been suborned by the presbyterians. Encouraged by them he probably was; but Huntington's memorial bears with it the stamp of truth, and it is confirmed by Cromwell's whole course of after-life.[45]

The independent party being the strongest, no advantage was made of these charges, which might otherwise have been deemed ground sufficient for depriving him of his command; and the ill-planned and ill-combined insurrection of the Cavaliers and invasion of the Scotch made him, as M. Villemain observes, too necessary to be deemed culpable. He marched first into Wales, and brought that crabbed expedition, as it was called, to a successful termination with his wonted celerity. That done, he proceeded against the Scotch, which, to the great furtherance of Cromwell's designs, Fairfax was not willing to do, for Fairfax had a sort of pyebald presbyterian conscience, and strained at a gnat now, after having bolted so many camels. Cromwell had a great dislike of the Scotch as well as a great contempt for them; he perfectly understood what their armies were, having served with them in one campaign, and therefore readily consented to go against them with a very inferior force. That confidence might have been fatal to him, if there had been common prudence in the duke of Hamilton and the other Scotch leaders; but the miserable creatures by whom the counsels of that army were directed chose to expose the English who were with them, instead of supporting them, when, by timely aid, the day might have been won. Cromwell declared he had never seen foot fight so desperately as the north-countrymen under Sir Marmaduke Langdale, at the battle of Preston, where

---

[45] Huntington's Complaint, dated 2d Aug., 1648, is printed in Thurloe's state papers, vol. i., pp. 94-97, and in vol. ii., of Maseres' tracts.

they were so basely left without support. They had their reward. Cromwell followed their army, defeated and routed it, more being killed out of contempt, says Clarendon, than that they deserved it by any opposition. He then marched to Edinburgh, where he was received as a deliverer; and settling the affairs of that lawless country under the management of Argyll, left it with reason to believe that it would prove as peaceable as he could wish.

The part which Cromwell bore in the tragedy that ensued, and the manner in which the hypocrisy, the coarseness, and the levity of his character were displayed, when, not having felt power or courage to prevent the wickedness, he took the lead in it himself, are known to all persons who have any knowledge of English history. The powers of Europe had most of them secretly fomented the rebellion, and made no attempt to avert the catastrophe which it brought about. France more especially had acted treacherously toward the king; commenting upon which, in the earlier part of his history, Lord Clarendon has some memorable observations upon the impolicy as well as the injustice of such conduct, "as if," he says, "the religion of princes were nothing but policy, and that they considered nothing more than to make all other kingdoms but their own miserable; and because God hath reserved them to be tried only within his own jurisdiction, that he means to try them too by other laws and rules than he hath published to the world for his servants to walk by. Whereas they ought to consider that God hath placed them over his people as examples, and to give countenance to his laws by their own strict observation of them; and that as their subjects are to be defended and protected by their princes, so they themselves are to be assisted and supported by one another, the function of kings being an order by itself; and as a contempt and breach of every law is in the policy of state an offence against the person of the king, because there is a kind of violation offered to his person in the transgression of that rule, without which he can not govern; so the rebellion of subjects against their prince ought to be looked upon by all other kings as an assault of their own sovereignty, and in some degree a design against monarchy itself, and consequently to be suppressed and extirpated, in what other kingdom soever it is, with the like concernment as if it were in their own bowels." Lord Bacon has noticed it as a defect in the historical part of learning that there is not an impartial and well attested *Historia Nemesios*. In such a history the miseries which France has undergone, and which Spain is undergoing and is to undergo, would exemplify the justice of Clarendon's remarks.

While other governments beheld the fate of Charles with an indifference as disreputable to their feelings as to their policy, and while the king of Spain adorned his palace by purchasing the choicest speciments of art with which Charles had enriched England, an honorable exception is to be made for Portugal and the house of Braganza. That house, in a time of extreme difficulty and danger, when it could ill afford to provoke another enemy, chose rather to incur the resentment and vengeance of the English commonwealth, than to refuse protection to Prince Rupert and the ships under his command; and when the parliamentary fleet entered the Tagus, and denounced war unless they were instantly delivered up, it was with difficulty that Prince Theodosius (whose untimely death may, perhaps, be considered as the greatest misfortune that ever befell the Portuguese) was dissuaded from going on board the Portuguese fleet himself, to join Prince Rupert, and give battle to his enemies. On that occasion the Braganzan family considered what was right and honorable, regardless of all meaner considerations; they supplied Rupert fully, and would not suffer his pursuers to leave the port till two tides after he had sailed out with a full gale. They suffered severely for this, but they preserved their honor; and as it behooves us not to forget this, so does it at this time especially behoove the Portuguese to remember in what manner the constant alliance and friendship of England, which for more than a hundred and sixty years has never been interrupted, was then deserved.

The levity which Cromwell displayed during that mockery of justice with which the king was sacrificed, Mr. Noble supposes to have been affected: and Mr. O. Cromwell endeavors to invalidate the evidence upon which it has been recorded and hitherto received. Its truth or falsehood would matter little in the fair estimate of his whole conduct, or of that particular act; and the thing itself is too consistent with other authentic anecdotes concerning him to be arbitrarily set aside. It is more remarkable that he went to look at the murdered king, opened the coffin himself, put his finger to the neck where it had been severed, and even inspecting the inside of the body, observed in how healthy a state it had been, and how well made for length of life. He had screwed his feelings as well as his conscience at this time to the sticking-place, and seems as if he had been resolved to make it known that he would shrink from nothing which might be necessary for his views. This was shown in the case of Lord Capel, a man in all respects of exemplary virtue, and worthy of the highest honors that history can bestow, as one who performed his duty faithfully, and to the last, in the worst of times. Cromwell knew him personally, spoke of him as of a friend, and made his very virtues a reason for taking away his life! His affection to the public, he said, so much weighed down his private friendship, that he could not but tell the house the question was whether they would preserve their most bitter and most implacable enemy; he knew the Lord Capel very well, and knew that he would be the last man in England who would forsake the royal interest; that he had great courage, industry, and generosity; that he had many friends who would always adhere to him; and that as long as he lived, what condition soever he was in, he would be a thorn in their sides; and therefore, for the good of the commonwealth, he should vote for his death. This was delivered and heard as a proof of republican virtue. God deliver us from all such virtues as harden the heart!

Hobbes has affirmed that at the time of Lord Capel's execution it was put to the question by army, whether all who had borne arms for the king should be massacred or no, and the noes carried it by only two voices.[46] If this be true, Cromwell, we may be sure, was one of those who declared against it; when he shed blood it was upon a calculating policy, never for the appetite of blood: such acts were committed by him against a good nature, not in the indulgence of a depraved one. Nor were the royalists the party of whom he was at that time most apprehensive; they were broken and dispersed, their cause was abandoned by man, and the pulpit incendiaries preached, and perhaps persuaded both themselves and others, that God had declared against it. The present danger was from the levellers, whom Cromwell had at first encouraged, and with whom it is very possible that in one stage of his progress he may sincerely have sympathized. But being now better acquainted with men and with things, his wish was to build up and repair the work of ruin; all further demolition was to be prevented, and therefore by prompt severity he suppressed these men, who were so numerous and well organized as to have rendered themselves formidable by their strength as well as by their opinions. That object having been effected, he accepted the command in Ireland, to the

---

[46] Arthur, Lord Capel, was executed 9th March, 1648.

surprise of his enemies, who desired nothing so much as his absence; not having considered that with his means and temper he went to a sure conquest, and must needs return from it with a great accession of popularity and power.

He arrived at Dublin [15th Aug., 1649] in a fortunate hour, just after the garrison had obtained a signal victory, in consequence of which the siege had been broken up. Without delay he marched against Drogheda,[47] where the Marquis of Ormond had placed a great number of his best troops, under Sir Arthur Aston, a brave and distinguished officer. One assault was manfully repulsed. Cromwell led his men a second time to the breach, who then forced all the retrenchments, and gave no quarter according to his positive orders. There was a great contention among the soldiers who should get the governor for his share of the spoil, because his artificial leg was believed to be made of gold; the disappointment at finding it only of wood was somewhat abated by discovering two hundred pieces of gold sewn up in his girdle. Cromwell's own account of the slaughter is, that not thirty of the whole number of the defendants escaped with their lives. "I do not believe," he says, "neither do I hear, that any officer escaped with his life, save only one lieutenant, who, going to the enemy, said he was the only man that escaped of all the garrison. The enemy were filled upon this with much terror, and truly I believe this bitterness will save much effusion of blood, through the goodness of God. I wish that all honest hearts may give the glory of this to God alone, to whom, indeed, the praise of this mercy belongs, for instruments they were very inconsiderable the work throughout." Lord Clarendon says that all manner of cruelty was executed; every Irish inhabitant, man, woman, and child, put to the sword, and three or four officers of name and of good families, whom some humaner soldiers concealed for four or five days, were then butchered in cold blood. Ludlow relates that the slaughter continued two days, and that such extraordinary severity was used to discourage others. Hugh Peters gave thanks for it in the cathedral at Dublin. The object was attained. Trim and Dundalk were abandoned to him without resistance; Wexford was ill defended and easily taken; and Cromwell, with a reliance upon fortune arising, in this instance, equally from confidence in himself and contempt of

---

[47] 3d Sept. 1649. He began his attack on the 9th. The battles of Dunbar and Worcester were fought on the 3d of September. He summoned a parliament on the 3d of September, and he died on the 3d of September.

his enemies, marched into Munster so far from all succor and all reasonable hope of supplies, that if the city of Cork had not been treacherously or pusillanimously given up to him, he and his army must have been reduced to the utmost danger.

In less than six months, though an infectious disease had broken out in his own army, Cromwell destroyed the last hopes of the royalists in Ireland, and exacted for a national crime, to which the massacre of St. Bartholomew's day is the only parallel in history, a vengeance to which no parallel can be found. No mercy was shown to any person who could be convicted of having shed protestant blood in that most merciless and atrocious rebellion. As many others as chose were allowed to enter into foreign services, and French and Spanish officers enlisted and transported not less than five and forty thousand men, though not five thousand could ever be raised for the king's service by all the unwearied exertions of Ormond, and all the promises and contracts which were made with him. Leaving Ireton with the command,[48] to pursue the war upon that system of extermination which the commonwealth intended, he obeyed the summons of parliament to put himself at the head of an army which was to march against Charles II., called at that time Charles Stuart, who was then in Scotland, in a situation something between that of a king and a prisoner. By Cromwell's desire the command was offered to Fairfax, who refused it, more because he was offended and ashamed at having discovered how mere a cipher he was become, than from any feeling of repentance for what he had done, and for what he had omitted to do, which was the heavier sin. In urging him to accept the command, Cromwell appeared so much in earnest that Ludlow believed him, and took him aside to entreat he would not in compliment and humility obstruct the service of the nation by his refusal. When it was determined that Cromwell was to be general, Ludlow had a conference with him, in which Cromwell professed to desire nothing more than that the government might be settled in a free and equal commonwealth, which he thought the only probable means of keeping out the old family. He looked upon it, he said, that the design of the Lord was now to free his people from every burden, and to accomplish what was prophesied in the 110th Psalm and then expounding that psalm for about an

---

[48] May, 1650. He arrived in London on the 31st. Whitlock, p.457, ed. 1732.

hour to Ludlow, and tickling him with expositions, professions, and praises, ended by letting him understand that if he pleased to accept the command of the horse in Ireland, the post would be at his service.[49]

A declaration was sent before Cromwell's army, addressed "to all that are saints, and partakers of the faith of God's elect in Scotland." The saints, however, in Scotland were praying and preaching against Cromwell as heartily as they had ever performed pulpit-service against Charles; and their presbyterian brethren in England, as well as the sober and untainted part of the people, were heartily wishing for his overthrow, and the return of the ancient order. His contempt for the Scotch had very nearly brought about the fulfilment of their desires: he got himself into a situation at Dunhar from which it was impossible to retreat, and where, from the want of provisions, the enemy must have had him at their mercy if they would only have avoided an action. But it was revealed to the preachers, by whom the general was controlled, that Agag was delivered into their hands; and Cromwell, perceiving them through his glass advancing to attack, exclaimed (in Hume's felicitous language) without the help of revelations, that the Lord had delivered them into *his*. Some of the preachers were knocked on the head while promising the victory, and others who were not killed "had very notable marks about the head and the face, that anybody might know, they were not hurt by chance, or in the crowd, but by very good will." A terrible execution was made; Cromwell's men gave no quarter till they were weary of killing. In his letter to the parliament he acknowledged the peril in which he had been, and that the enemy had reminded him of the fate of Essex's army in Cornwall; "but," says he, "in what they were thus lifted up, the Lord was above them. The enemy having these advantages, we lay very near him, being sensible of our disadvantages, having some weakness of flesh, but yet consolation and support from the Lord himself to our poor weak faith (wherein I believe not a few among us stand), that because of their numbers, because of their advantages, because of their confidence, because of our weakness, because of our strait, we were on the mount, and on the mount the Lord would be seen." And he adds that the Lord of hosts made them as stubble to their swords.

---

[49] Ludlow's Memoirs, ed. 1771 pp. 136-'7

The battle of Dunbar (3d Sept. 1650) delivered Charles from the tyranny of the presbyterians, who, he verily believed, would have imprisoned him the next day if they had won the victory. Cromwell entered Edinburgh: the castle was surrendered to him, and he was soon master of the better part of the kingdom; but he had a severe, illness, with three relapses, and was in great danger. His reply, after his recovery, to a letter of inquiry from the lord president of the council of state in England, acknowledged, with all humble thankfulness, their high favor in sending to inquire after one so unworthy as himself. "Indeed, my lord," he continues, "your service needs not me; I am a poor creature, and have been a dry bone, and am still an unprofitable servant to my Master and you. I thought I should have died of this fit of sickness, but the Lord seemeth to dispose otherwise. But truly, my lord, I desire not to live unless I may obtain mercy from the Lord, to approve my heart and life to him in more faithfulness and thankfulness, and those I serve with more profitableness and diligence" When he was well enough to take the field, and advance against the king at Stirling, a skilful movement, by which he got behind the royal army, thereby cutting it off from the fruitful country whence it drew its supplies, induced Charles to form the brave resolution of marching into England.

Cromwell had not expected this; and when he announced it to the parliament, it was with something like an apology for himself, though he said the enemy had taken this course in desperation and fear, and out of inevitable necessity. "I do apprehend," he says, "that it will trouble some men's thoughts, and may occasion some inconveniences, of which I hope we are as deeply sensible, and have, and I trust shall be as diligent to prevent as any. And indeed this is our comfort, that in simplicity of heart as to God, we have done to the best of our judgments, knowing that if some issue were not put to this business, it would occasion another winter's war, to the ruin of your soldiery, for whom the Scots are too hard, in respect of enduring the winter difficulties of this country. We have this comfortable experiment from the Lord, that this enemy is heart-smitten by God, and whenever the Lord shall bring us up to them, we believe the Lord will make the desperateness of this counsel of theirs to appear, and the folly of it also." The alarm in London was very great. "Both the city and the country," says Mrs. Hutchinson, "were all amazed, doubtful of their own and the commonwealth's safety. Some could not hide very pale and unmanly fears, and were in such distraction of spirit as much disturbed their councils." Even Bradshaw, "stout-hearted as he was," trembled for his neck. But great exertions were made by the government, its members having indeed everything at stake, and Whitelock says that no "affair could have been managed with more diligence, courage, and prudence; and that peradventure there was never so great a body of men, so well armed and provided, got together in so short a time, as were those sent to reinforce Cromwell." Cromwell meantime followed the royal army with his wonted confidence. Whatever his military skill may have been, he possessed in perfection two of the first requisites for a general, activity and decision; while in the king's councils he knew that there would be conflicting opinions, vacillations, delay, and imbecility. When therefore he came to Worcester, advantageous as that position was to the enemy if they had known how to profit by it, he marched directly on as to a prey; and not troubling himself with the formality of a siege, ordered his troops to fall on in all places at once. According to his own account, the loss on his side did not exceed two hundred men; yet it was, he said, "a stiff business,"—"as stiff a contest for four or five hours as ever he had seen." The royal army was completely routed and dispersed; and the victory was the more gratifying to Cromwell on account of its being achieved on the anniversary of the battle of Dunbar. In his letter to the parliament he says, "the dimensions of this mercy are above my thoughts; it is, for aught I know, a crowning mercy. I am bold humbly to beg that all thoughts may tend to the promoting of his honor who hath wrought so great salvation; and that the fatness of these continued mercies may not occasion pride and wantonness, as formerly the like hath done to a chosen nation."

The defeat of Charles at Worcester (3d Sept., 1651) is one of those events which most strikingly exemplify how much better events are disposed of by Providence than they would be if the direction were left to the choice even of the best and the wisest men. Had the victory been on the king's side, other battles must have been fought; his final success could not have been attained without a severe struggle; a second contest would have arisen among his own friends, between the members of the church and the presbyterians, which might probably have kindled another civil war; and the puritans, and their descendants to this day, would have insisted that if the commonwealth had not been overthrown, the continuance of that free and liberal government would richly have repaid the country for all its sufferings. But by the battle of Worcester, the commonwealth's men were left absolute masters of the three kingdoms; they had full leisure to complete and perfect their own structure of government: the experiment was fairly tried; there was nothing from without to disturb the process; it went duly on from change to change, from one evil to another; anarchy in its certain consequences leading to military despotism; that again, when the sword was no longer wielded by a strong hand, giving place to anarchy till the people, at length weary of their sufferings and their insecurity, while knaves and fanatics were contending for the mastery over them, restored the monarchy with one consent.

When Cromwell called the battle of Worcester a *crowning* mercy, he may have used that word in a double sense between pun and prophecy; for certain it is that from this time he did not conceal the kingly thoughts and views which he entertained. He would have knighted Lambert and Fleetwood upon the field, if his friends had not dissuaded him; and soon afterward, when Ireton's death delivered him from the only person whom he regarded with deference, he assembled certain members of parliament, with some of the chief officers, at the speaker's house, told them it was necessary to come to a settlement of the nation, and delivered his own opinion in favor of a settlement with somewhat of a monarchical power in it. The lawyers who were present were in general for a mixed monarchy; and many were for choosing the duke of Gloucester king, who was still in their hands, and was, as they said, too young to have borne arms against them, or to be infected with the principles of their enemies. The officers were as generally against monarchy, though every one of them, says Whitelock, was a monarch in his regiment or company. For the present, Cromwell was satisfied with having felt his ground, and waited while the Long parliament made themselves more and more odious by the desire which they manifested of perpetuating their own power, the war, which they provoked with the Dutch, and the severities which they exercised by their abominable high court of justice, where tools of the ruling party, who had no character to lose, acted at once as judge and jury. The prisoners taken at Worcester were driven like cattle to London; many of them perished there in confinement for want of food, and the rest were sold to the plantations for slaves by the despotic government which had risen upon the ruins of the throne! This act of abominable tyranny is mentioned by

Baxter without any comment, and apparently without the slightest feeling. But when he relates that Mr. Love, one of the London ministers, was condemned and beheaded by the same authority—then, indeed, heaven and earth are moved at such an enormity! "At the time of his execution, or very near it on that day, there was the dreadfulest thunder, and lightning, and tempest, that was heard or seen for a long time before. This blow sunk deeper toward the root of the new commonwealth than will easily be believed, and made them grow odious to almost all the religious party in the land except the sectaries. And there is, as Sir Walter Raleigh noteth of learned men, such as Demosthenes, Cicero, &c., so much more in divines of famous learning and piety, enough to put an everlasting odium upon those whom they suffer by, though the cause of the sufferers were not justifiable. Men count him a vile and detestable creature, who in his passion, or for his interest, or any such low account, shall deprive the world of such lights and ornaments, and cut off so much excellency at a blow.—After this the most of the ministers and good people of the land did look upon the new commonwealth as tyranny."

The Long parliament having made itself as much hated by the presbyterians as it was by the royalists, was odious at the same time to the army and the fanatics of both kinds, political and religious. Cromwell stated their misconduct to Whitelock strongly, and with none of that muddiness with which he frequently chose to conceal or obscure his meaning. On this occasion he spoke plainly: "Their pride," he said, "and ambition and self-seeking, engrossing all places of honor and profit to themselves and their friends; and their daily breaking forth into new and violent parties and factions: their delays of business, and design to perpetuate themselves and to continue their power in their own hands; their meddling in private matters between party and party, contrary to the institution of parliaments, and their injustice and partiality in those matters, and the scandalous lives of some of the chief of them—these things do give too much ground for people to open their mouths against them and to dislike them. Nor can they be kept within the bounds of justice and law or reason, they themselves being the supreme power of the nation, liable to no account to any, nor to be controlled or regulated by any other power; there being none superior or co-ordinate with them." Whitelock confessed the evil, but said it would be hard to find a remedy. "What," said Cromwell, "if a man should take upon him to be king?"

To this Whitelock replied that this remedy would be worse than the disease; that being general he had less envy and less danger than if he were called king, but not less power and real opportunities of doing good. And he represented to him that he was environed with secret enemies: that his own officers were elated with success; "many of them," said he, "are busy and of turbulent spirits, and are not without their designs how they may dismount your excellency, and some of themselves get up into the saddle—how they may bring you down and set up themselves." Cromwell would willingly have engaged Whitelock in his views; but Whitelock was a cautious, temporising man, who generally chose the safest part, and never incurred danger by resisting what he could not prevent, or putting himself in the van when he could remain with the main body. In speaking honestly to Cromwell, he risked nothing; the feeling which his dissent excited was rather disappointment than displeasure, and he would be esteemed more for his sincerity.[50]

His concurrence was of little moment. Cromwell could count upon his faithful services when the thing was done, and he had plenty of other agents who were ready to go through with any thing. That memorable scene soon followed (20th April, 1653), when Cromwell turned out the parliament, and locked the doors of the house of commons. Whitelock says, that "all honest and prudent indifferent men were highly distasted at this; that the royalists rejoiced;

---

[50] See the whole of this remarkable conversation in Whitelock, pp. 548-551, ed. 1732.

"Whitelock was a man who, taking at first, in honest conviction, what is called the patriotic aside, adhered to it when men as honest as himself, of far higher intellectual powers, and greater moral courage, went over to the king's party. He conformed to all changes during the course of the rebellion, not from any greedy or ambitious views, but because he hoped that every change might be the last, and dreaded the danger of any attempt at restoring that order of things which had been by violence subverted. The weight of his respectable character was thus thrown into whatever scale preponderated. But in all other respects he was so estimable a man—never injuring others, and seeking only to secure, not to aggrandize, himself—that the royalists regarded him with no asperity; they looked upon his conduct as proceeding entirely from moral timidity, unmixed with any worse motive; and when he appeared at Charles II.'s court, to make his excuses, the king, with that good-nature which—though it was far from covering the multitude of his sins—gave a grace to much that he did and to everything he said, bade him go home and take care of his fourteen children."— SOUTHEY, *Letter to John Murray, Esq, "touching" Lord Nugent*, p. 31.

that divers fierce men, pastors of churches and their congregations, were pleased," as were the army in general, officers as well as soldiers; and he illustrates the principles upon which some of the officers were pleased with the change, by what one of them said to a member of the ejected parliament, whose son was a captain, that "this business was nothing but to pull down the father and set up the son, and no more but for the father to wear worsted, and the son silk stockings,"—so sottish, says Whitelock, were they in the apprehensions of their own risings![51]—but he has not thought proper to observe, how much more sottish and less excusable were those persons who had set them the example of pulling down authority. Some of the severest republicans in the army served Cromwell in this his first act of explicit despotism. Ludlow, who was in Ireland, had some distrust; yet, he says that he and they who were with them thought themselves obliged, by the rules of charity, to hope the best, and, therefore, continued to act in their places and stations as before. They had never exercised that rule of charity toward Charles I.

The lord general, such was his title now, called a meeting of officers to deliberate concerning what should next be done. Lambert was for intrusting the supreme power to a few persons, not more than ten or twelve. Harrison would have preferred seventy, being the number of which the Jewish Sanhedrim consisted. The deliberation ended in summoning[52] to a parliament a hundred and twenty-eight persons chosen by the council of officers, from the three kingdoms. The members thus curiously chosen, and notorious by the name of Praise-God Barebones' parliament, met accordingly (4th July, 1653), and were harangued by Cromwell, who acknowledged the goodness of the Lord, in that he then saw the day wherein the saints began their rule in the earth! They began their business in a saintly manner, by "a day of humiliation in which God did so draw forth the hearts of the members both in speaking and prayer, that they did not find any necessity to call for the help of any minister." They were, indeed, for dispensing with ministers as well as kings, looking upon the function as anti-christian, and upon tithes as absolute Judaism; and the better to insure the abolition of that odious order, they proposed to sell all the college lands, and apply the money in aid of taxes. It had been intended that they should sit fifteen months, and that, three months

---

[51] Whitelock, p. 555, ed. 1732.
[52] 8th June, 1653. See a summons in Whitelock, p. 557.

before their dissolution, they should make choice of others to succeed them for a year, the three kingdoms being then to be governed by each electing its successor. Five months, however, convinced Cromwell that the only use to be made of them was, to make them surrender their power into his hand, acknowledge their own insufficiency (which they might do with perfect truth), and beseech him to take care of the commonwealth. The council of officers were now again in possession of the supreme power; and they declared that the government of the commonwealth should reside in the single person of Oliver Cromwell, with the title of lord protector, and a council of one-and-twenty to assist him.[53]

Constitutions were made in that age as easily as in this, and the articles were not more durable then than they are now, though wiser heads were employed in making them. The name, however, which Oliver chose for his piece of parchment was the Instrument of Government.[54] It was there ordained, that the protector should call a parliament once in every three years, and not dissolve it till it had sat five months; that the bills which were presented to him, if he did not confirm them within twenty days, should become laws without his confirmation; and his select council should not be more in number than twenty-one, nor less than thirteen; that with their consent, he might make laws which should be binding during the intervals of parliament; that he should have power to make peace and war; that immediately after his death, the council should choose another protector, and that no protector after him should be general of the army. The first use which he made of his power was to make peace with the Dutch and with Portugal, in both cases upon terms honorable and advantageous to England; nor could any measures have been more popular than these, which delivered the nation in the first instance from an expensive and bloody contest, and in the other, restored to it its most productive foreign trade. France and Spain were emulously courting the friendship of the fortunate usurper: Ireland and Scotland thoroughly subdued, their governments united with that of England, by the right of conquest, and both countries undergoing that process of civilization which Cromwell, like the Romans, carried on by the sword. When Charles I., was

---

[53] He was installed lord protector 16th December, 1653, and proclaimed the 19th. The Barebones' parliament ended 12th December, 1653.

[54] See at length in Whitelock, pp. 571-577, ed. 1732.

treating with the Scotch, before he put himself into their hands, he said in a letter to the French agent, whom they authorized to promise him protection, "Let them never flatter themselves so with their good successes; without pretending to prophecy, I will foretell their ruin, except they agree with me, however it shall please God to dispose of me." They had reason to remember this when they were under Cromwell's government. His orders to Monk, whom he left to complete the subjugation of the country, were, that if he found a stubborn resistance at any place, he should give no quarter, and allow free plunder; orders which Monk observed with the utmost rigor, and "made himself as terrible as man could be."[55] "He subdued them," says Clarendon, "to all imaginable tameness, though he had exercised no other power over them than was necessary to reduce that people to an entire submission to that tyrannical yoke. In all his other carriage toward them, but what was in order to that end, he was friendly and companionable enough; and as he was feared by the nobility and hated by the clergy, so he was not unloved by the common people, who received more justice and less oppression from him, than they had been accustomed to under their own lords." A more thorough conquest was never effected: everything was changed, the whole frame of government new-modelled, the Kirk subjected to the sole order and direction of the commander-in-chief; the nobles stripped of their power; the very priests tamed and muzzled—and all this was submitted to obediently!—in reality, it had brought with it so much real benefit to a barbarous people, that at the restoration, Lord Clarendon admits "it might well be a question, whether the generality of the nation was not better contented with it than to return into the old road of subjection."

A more rigorous system had been pursued in Ireland, a system severer than even the mode of Roman civilization. The utter extirpation of the Irish had been intended! but this was found "to be in itself very difficult, and to carry in it somewhat of horror, that made some impression upon the stone-hardness of their own hearts." The act of grace (so it was called!) for which this purpose was commuted, was the most desperate remedy that ever was applied to a desperate disease. All the Irish who had survived the ravages of fire, sword, famine, and pestilence, and who had not transported themselves, were

---

[55] Clar. Hist., vi., 494, ed. 1826.

compelled, by a certain day, to retire within a certain part of the province of Connaught, the most barren of the island, and at that time almost desolate; after that time, if man, woman, or child, of that unhappy generation, were found beyond the limits, they were to be killed like wild beasts; the land within that circuit was to be divided among them, and the rest of the island was portioned out among the conquerors, who used the right of conquest with greater severity than Romans, Saxons, or Normans, had exercised in Britain. It is worthy of remark, that not a voice was heard against this tremendous act of oppression, such horror had the Irish massacre excited, and so irreclaimable, in the judgment of all men, was the nature of the inhabitants: even when new settlers established themselves there, "though what virtue of the soil," says Harrington, "or vice of the air soever it be, they came still to degenerate:" and of the descendants of English colonists there, it was said in Elizabeth's time, that they were *Hibernis ipsis Hiberniores.* So little were their rights, or even their existence, taken into the account, that Harrington thought the best thing the commonwealth could do with Ireland was to farm it to the Jews for ever, for the pay of an army to protect them during the first seven years, and two millions a year from that time forward!—What was to be done with the Irish, whether they were to be made hewers of wood and drawers of water, or to become Jews by compulsion, he has not explained. For the sufferings of the Irish, however, Cromwell is not responsible; and under the order which he established, if it had continued for another generation, the island would have been in a better state than any which its authentic history has yet recorded: for there, as in Scotland, a more equitable administration was introduced than that which had been destroyed.

While the protector was feared and respected by foreign powers, and obeyed submissively, if not willingly, in Ireland and the sister kingdom, his state at home was full of uneasiness and danger. Though orders were given, when he summoned his first parliament, that no persons should be chosen who had borne arms on the king's part, nor the sons of any such, and though care was taken to return such members as were believed to be the best affected to his government, yet in the first debate his authority was questioned; and one member declared that, "for his own part, as God had made him instrumental in cutting down tyranny in one person, so now he could not endure to see the nation's liberties shackled by another, whose right to the government could not be measured otherwise than by the length of his sword, which alone had emboldened him to command his commanders." He attempted to curb this spirit, by excluding all who would not subscribe an engagement to be true and faithful to the Lord protector; yet they who took the engagement were found so impracticable for his purposes, that, taking advantage of the letter of his instrument, he dissolved them at the end of five *lunar* months.

Cromwell was now paying the bitter price of successful ambition. His good sense and his good nature would have led him to govern equitably and mercifully, to promote literature, to cherish the arts, and to pour wine and oil into the wounds of the nation. But as, in the language of the schools, *uno absurdo dato, sequuntur millia,* so in politics and in morals, are error and guilt fearfully prolific: the disease of the root taints the remotest branches. Having attained to power by sinister means, Cromwell, in spite of himself, was compelled to govern tyrannically; he was equally in danger from the royalists, the greater though inactive part of the nation, among whom indignant spirits were continually at work, and from the levellers, by whose instrumentality he had raised himself to his insecure and miserable elevation. He could not rely even upon the officers of that army by which alone he was supported; and he had so little confidence in the soldiers, that he once intended to bring over a Swiss regiment as a guard for his own person, and had sent an agent to take measures for raising it; but having perceived how unpopular such a manifestation of his fears would be, and how dangerous, he was deterred from his purpose. His best security was in the irreconcileable difference between the royalists and the fanatics, the latter willingly aiding him to oppress the former, of whom he stood most in fear. It was confidently affirmed, that the proposal for massacring the whole royal party was more than once brought forward in his council of officers, as the only expedient to secure the government; but Cromwell, who was neither devil enough to commit the crime, nor fool enough to destroy the balance by which he was preserved, never would consent. The royalists, in other respects, had little reason to praise his moderation. After all the plunder and exactions which they had suffered, and the *compositions* which they had paid for their own estates, Cromwell now, by his own authority and that of his council, issued an order for decimating their estates, that is, that they should pay a tenth, not of the income, but of the value of the property; and a declaration accompanied this order, that, because of their inherent malignity, they must not wonder if they were looked upon as a common enemy; and that they "must not expect to be prosecuted like other men, by the ordinary forms of justice, and to have the crimes proved by witnesses, before they should be concluded to be guilty." If the loyal part of the people had at first lent the king the fifth part of what, after infinite losses, they were compelled to sacrifice to his enemies at last, Lord Clarendon says, that Charles would have been enabled to preserve them and himself. "The Lord deliver us," says Laud, "from covetous and fearful men! The covetous will betray us for money, the fearful for security." He did not live to see how the persons, who acted under the influence of these base passions, brought upon themselves worse evils than could have befallen them in the manly discharge of their duties.

The better to exact this forced payment, and with a view, also, toward imbodying a sort of national army, which might be employed in case of need to balance or repress the troops, whose fidelity he distrusted, he divided England into twelve cantons, each of which was placed under the absolute power of a major-general. These bashaws, as Ludlow calls them, were to levy all imposts, sequester those who did not pay the decimation, and commit to prison any persons whom they suspected; and there was no appeal from any of their acts, but to the protector. In each canton he raised a body of horse and foot, who were only to be called out in cases of necessity, and then to serve a certain number of days at their own charge; if they served longer, they were to receive the same pay as the army, but they were to be under the major-general of their respective canton. A certain salary was allowed them, that of a horseman being eight pounds a year. But the advantage which he might have derived from this kind of yeomanry force (that of all other which may most reasonably be depended upon for the preservation of order), brought with it a new danger from the power of the majors-general; and Cromwell removed these bashaws in time, without difficulty, because they had made themselves odious to the nation.

He called his next parliament[56] with more confidence, because the war in which he had engaged against Spain had made him master of Jamaica, and two

---

[56] 3d September, 1654, dissolved 31st January, 1654-'5.

treasure-ships, with a frightful destruction of the Spaniards, had been taken. The treasure was brought in wagons from Portsmouth to London, and paraded through the city to the Tower. Most of the members took the test which he required; they passed an act binding all men to renounce Charles Stuart and his family; they declared it high treason to attempt the life of the protector, and granted him larger supplies than had ever before been raised, one of the imposts being a full year's rent upon all houses which had been erected in and about London, from before the beginning of the troubles. Finally, they offered him the title of king, which was the great object of his ambition. The republicans, from whom he expected most danger, had been carefully excluded by management in the elections, or by the test. Vane and Harrison were in confinement, for Cromwell feared the craft of the former, and the enthusiasm of the latter, which placed him above all means of corruption or intimidation. Yet there was more opposition than he had anticipated; and one member applied to him in the house, the words of the prophet to Ahab, "Hast thou killed and also taken possession?" Lambert, who had hitherto forwarded all the views of Oliver, because he expected to be the next protector himself, being the second man in the army, declared against a proposal which would have been fatal to his ambition: and there were members bold enough to say, that if they must submit to the old government, they would much rather choose to obey the true and lawful heir of a long line of kings, than one who was but at best their equal, and had raised himself by the trust which they had reposed in him. Upon such opposition Cromwell would have trampled, if he had found support in his own family and nearest connexions. But his sons were without ambition. Richard, the eldest, indeed was believed to be at heart a royalist; Desborough, who had married his sister, and Fleetwood, who was his son-in-law (having married Ireton's widow), with a stupid obstinacy objected to his assuming the name of king, though they had no objection to his exercising a more absolute authority than any king of England had ever possessed. Colonel Pride, who had purged the parliament to make him what he was, procured a petition from the majority of the officers then about London, against his taking the title; and information, to which he game full credit, was conveyed to him, that a number of men had bound themselves by oath to kill him, within so many hours after he should accept it. Under these disheartening circumstances, after a long and painful struggle with himself, and some curious discussions with the deputation of members, who were sent to urge his acceptance, he concluded by refusing it upon the plea of conscience.[57]

In thus yielding to men of weaker minds than his own, Cromwell committed the same error which had been fatal to Charles. The boldest course would have been the safest; the wisest friends of the royal family were of opinion, that if he had made himself king *de facto*, and restored all things in other respects to the former order, no other measure would have been so injurious to the royal cause. Everything except the name was given him; the power of appointing his successor in the protectorship was now conferred upon him by parliament, and the ceremony of investitute was performed for the second time, and with a pomp which no coronation had exceeded. The speaker presented him with a robe of purple velvet, a mixed color, to show the mixture of justice and mercy, which he was to observe in his administration; the bible, "the book of books, in which the orator told him he had the happiness to be well versed, and which contained both precepts and examples for good government;" a sceptre, not unlike a staff, for he was to be a staff to the weak and poor; and lastly, a sword, not to defend himself alone, but his people also: "If," said the speaker, "I might presume to fix a motto upon this sword, as the valiant Lord Talbot had upon his, it should be this: *Ego sum Domini Protectoris, ad protegendum populum meum*—I am the Lord Protector's, to protect my people."

So great was the reputation which Cromwell obtained abroad by his prodigious elevation, the lofty tone of his government, and the vigor of his arms, that an Asiatic Jew is said to have come to England for the purpose of investigating his pedigree, thinking to discover in him the lion of the tribe of Judah! Some of his own most faithful adherents regarded him with little less veneration. Their warm attachment, and the more doubtful devotion of a set of enthusiastic preachers, drugged the atmosphere in which he breathed; and yet, white his bodily health continued, the natural strength of his understanding prevailed over this deleterious influence, and he saw things calmly, clearly, and sorrowfully, as they were. Shakspere himself has not imagined a more dramatic situation than that in which Cromwell stood. He

---

[57] 8th May, 1657. On the 16th December, 1653, he was installed lord protector, and on the 26th June, 1657, inaugurated lord protector. Whitelock, p. 571 and p. 662, ed. 1732.

had attained to the possession of sovereign power, by means little less guilty than Macbeth, but the process had neither hardened his heart, nor made him desperate in guilt. His mind had expanded with his fortune. As he advanced in his career, he gradually discovered how mistaken he had been in the principles upon which he had set out; and, after having effected the overthrow of the church, the nobles, and the throne, he became convinced, by what experience (the surest of all teachers) had shown him, that episcopacy, nobility, and monarchy, were institutions good in themselves, and necessary for this nation in which they had so long been established. Fain would he have repaired the evil which he had done; fain would he have restored the monarchy, created a house of peers, and re-established the episcopal church. But he was thwarted and overruled by the very instruments which he had hitherto used; men whom he had formerly possessed with his own passionate errors, and whom he was not able to dispossess: persons incapable of deriving wisdom from experience, and so short-sighted as not to see that their own lives and fortunes depended upon the establishment of his power by the only means which could render it stable and secure. Standing in fear of them, he dared not take the crown himself; and he could not confer upon the rightful heir:—by the murder of Charles, he had incapacitated himself from making that reparation which would otherwise have been in his power. His wife, who was not elated with prosperity, advised him to make terms with the exiled king, and restore him to the throne; his melancholy answer was, "Charles Stuart can never forgive me his father's death; and if he could, he is unworthy of the crown." He answered to the same effect, when the same thing was twice proposed to him, with the condition that Charles should marry one of his daughters. What would not Cromwell have given, whether he looked to this world or the next, if his hands and been clear of the king's blood!

Such was the state of Cromwell's mind during the latter years of his life, when he was lord of these three kingdoms, and indisputably the most powerful potentate in Europe, and as certainly the greatest man of an age in which the race of great men was not extinct in any country. No man was so worthy of the station which he filled, had it not been for the means by which he reached it. He would have governed constitutionally, mildly, mercifully, liberally, if he could have followed the impulses of his own heart, and the wishes of his better mind; self-preservation compelled him to a severe and suspicious system: he was reduced at last to govern without a parliament, because, pack them and purge them as he might, all that he summoned proved unmanageable; and because he was a usurper, he became of necessity a despot. The very saints, in whose eyes he had been so precious, now called him an "ugly tyrant," and engaged against him in more desperate plots than were formed by the royalists. He lived in perpetual danger and in perpetual fear. When he went abroad he was surrounded by his guards. It was never known which way he was going till he was in the coach; he seldom returned by the same way he went; he wore armor under his clothes, and hardly ever slept two nights successively in one chamber. The latter days of Charles, while he looked on to the scaffold, and endured the insolence of Bradshaw and the inhuman aspersions of Cook, were enviable when compared to the close of Cromwell's life. Charles had that peace within which passeth all understanding; the one great sin which he had committed in sacrificing Strafford had been to him a perpetual cause of sorrow and shame and repentance; he received his own death as a just punishment for that sin under the dispensations of a righteous and unerring Providence; and feeling that it had been expiated, when he bowed his head upon the block, it was in full reliance upon the justice of posterity, and with a sure and certain trust in the mercy of his God. Cromwell had doubts of both. Ludlow tells us, that at his death "he seemed, above all, concerned for the reproaches, he said, men would cast upon his name, in trampling on his ashes when dead!" And the last sane feeling of religion which he expressed implied a like misgiving, concerning his condition in the world on which he was about to enter—it was a question to one of his fanatical preachers,[58] "if the doctrine were true, that the elect could never finally fall?" Upon receiving a reply, that nothing could be more certain, "Then am I safe," he said, "for I am sure that *once* I was in a state of grace." The spiritual drams which were then administered to him in strong doses, acted powerfully upon a mind debilitated by long disease, and disposed by the nature of that disease to delirium. He assured his physicians, as the presumptuous fanatics by whom he was surrounded assured him, that he should not die, whatever they might think from the symptoms of his disorder, for God was far above nature, and God had promised his recovery. Thanks were publicly given for the

---

[58] John Goodwin.

undoubted pledges of his recovery, which God had vouchsafed! and some of his last words were those of a mediator rather than a sinner, praying for the people, as if his own merits entitled him to be an intercessor. Even his death did not dissipate the delusion. When that news was brought to those who were met together to pray for him, "Mr. Sterry stood up and desired them not to be troubled: for," said he, "this is good news! because, if he was of great use to the people of God when he was among us, now he will be much more so, being ascended to heaven to sit at the right hand of Jesus Christ, there to intercede for us, and to be mindful of us on all occasions!"[59]

The life of this most fortunate and least flagitious of usurpers might hold out a salutary lesson for men possessed with a like ambition, if such men were capable of learning good as well as evil lessons from the experience of others. He gained three kingdoms; the price which he paid for them was innocence and peace of mind. He left an imperishable name, so stained with reproach, that notwithstanding the redeeming virtues which adorned him, it were better for him to be forgotten than to be so remembered. And in the world to come ———— but it is not for us to anticipate the judgments, still less to limit the mercy, of the All-merciful.

Let us repeat, that there is no portion of history in which it so much behooves an Englishman to be thoroughly versed as in that of Cromwell's age. There it may be seen to what desperate lengths men of good hearts and laudable intentions may be drawn by faction. There may be seen the rise, and the progress, and the consequences of rebellion. There are to be found the highest examples of true patriotism, sound principles, and heroic virtue, with some alloy of haughtiness in Strafford, of human infirmities in Laud, pure and unsullied in Falkland, and Capel, and Newcastle, and in Clarendon, the wisest and the best of English statesmen, the most authentic, the most candid, the most instructive of English historians. From the history of that age, and more especially from that excellent writer, the young and ingenuous may derive and

---

[59] Cromwell died in a whirlwind, on the 3d September, 1658. On the 23d November, he was buried in Henry VII.'s chapel with more than regal solemnity. At the restoration his body was taken up and hung at Tyburn. Forty years afterward, Dryden alludes to the storm in which the protector died, in a letter to his cousin, Mrs. Steward. Many of the large trees in St. James's park were torn up by the roots.

He was taken ill at Hampton court, and died at Whitehall.

confirm a just, and generous, and ennobling love for the institutions of their country, founded upon the best feelings and surest principles; and the good and the thoughtful of all ages will feel in the perusal, with what reason that petition is inserted in the Litany, wherein we pray the Lord to deliver us "from all sedition, privy conspiracy, and rebellion; from all false doctrine, heresy, and schism: from hardness of heart and contempt of his word and commandments,"—sins which draw after them, in certain and inevitable consequence, the heaviest of all chastisements upon a guilty nation.[60]

THE END.

---

[60] After the murder of the king change followed change, but no change brought stability to the state, or repose to the nation, not even when the supreme and absolute authority was usurped by a man who of all others was the most worthy to have exercised it, had it lawfully devolved upon him. Cromwell relieved the country from presbyterian intolerance; and he curbed those fanatics who were for proclaiming king Jesus, that, as his saints, they might divide the land among themselves. But it required all his strength to do this, and to keep down the spirit of political and religious fanaticism, when his own mind by its own strength had shaken off both diseases. He then saw and understood the beauty, and the utility, and the necessity of those establishments, civil and ecclesiastical, over the ruins of which he had made his way to power; and gladly would he have restored the monarchy and the episcopal church. But he was deterred from the only practicable course, less by the danger of the attempt than by the guilty part which he had borne in the king's fate; and at the time when Europe regarded him with terror and admiration as the ablest and most powerful potentate of the age, he was paying the bitter penalty of successful ambition, consumed by cares and anxieties, and secret fears, and only preserved from all the horrors of remorse by the spiritual drams which were administered to him as long as he had life.—SOUTHEY, *Book of the Church*, ed. 1841, p. 509.

www.ingramcontent.com/pod-product-compliance
Lightning Source LLC
Chambersburg PA
CBHW020430010526
44118CB00010B/508